I0815856

PRESENTED TO

..............................................................................................

BY

..............................................................................................

ON THE OCCASION OF

..............................................................................................

DATE

..............................................................................................

# THE GREAT OUTDOORS DEVOTIONAL

# THE GREAT OUTDOORS DEVOTIONAL

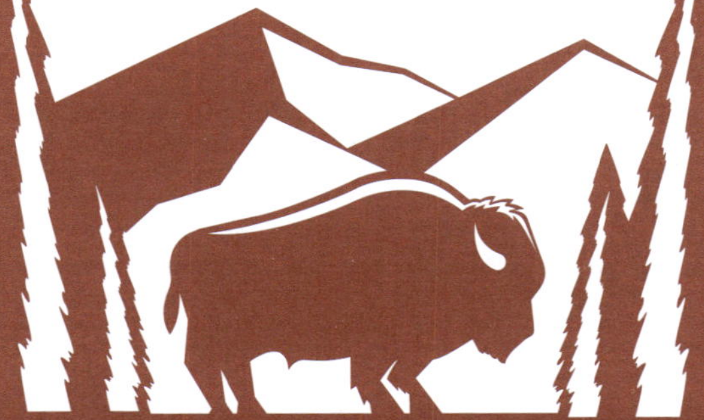

100 READINGS

FOR GUYS WHO LOVE GOD'S CREATION

ISBN 978-1-63609-878-4



Cover Design: Greg Jackson, Thinkpen Design

Published by Barbour Publishing, Inc., 1810 Barbour Drive, Uhrichsville, Ohio 44683, www.barbourbooks.com

*Our mission is to inspire the world with the life-changing message of the Bible.*

Printed in China.

# — 1 —

# STARTING OUT SMALL

*For you see your calling, brothers,*
*how not many wise men according to the flesh,*
*not many mighty, not many noble are called.*
1 Corinthians 1:26 SKJV

Near Yosemite National Park stands a grove of old-growth trees, rising like lofty towers, lifting their arms to heaven all day long.

These mammoth trees are hundreds of years old, having weathered fire and famine, parasites and people. Look around, and you'll see other, smaller trees—about the size of a person—dotting the area. There's nothing special about them: their slender trunks contrast sharply with the breathtaking girth of the colossal trees nearby. But every giant in the grove started out just like those young trees.

As Christians, we too have a towering destiny ahead of us. The contrast between what we are now and what we've been called to seems too large to fathom. But God intentionally chose the weak, not the mighty, for great things. Let's look ahead with anticipation, boasting now of what the Lord will do.

## FOR FURTHER THOUGHT

The age of a tree can be determined by its "tree rings"—markings left behind from years of growth. What are some spiritual tree rings in your life?

Every "mighty oak" in the Bible—each person of strength and courage—started out as a mere sapling. Which of these heroes' journeys does your life resemble so far?

## PRAYER

*Unfathomable God, thank You for Your ability to produce power from weakness. Work in my life today, nurturing my spirit with Your love and strength.*

## — 2 —

# FROM THE DEPTHS OF THE EARTH

*You who have made me see many troubles and calamities will revive me again; from the depths of the earth you will bring me up again.*

PSALM 71:20 ESV

Mammoth Cave, in Kentucky, is the world's largest cave system. It has over 360 miles of tunnels and is still not fully explored and mapped.

As spelunkers walk, crawl, and wiggle through its maze of twisting little passages, all seemingly alike, claustrophobia begins setting in. And when the light blinks out, this unsettling fear can easily morph into mind-numbing panic. All of the once-clear sights and landmarks become one with the perfect blackness.

Isn't life often like the Mammoth Cave? Have you ever,

by your own free will, descended too far into sin, losing sight of your way out?

God sometimes allows us to get into trouble. But He will never be far from us. To escape, all we need is the light.

## FOR FURTHER THOUGHT

For some, the darkness of sin's cave is all they've ever known. How can we as Christians persuade them of the beauty of the light?

What are some scripture verses that serve as flashlights in an otherwise pitch-black environment? Have you committed them to memory?

## PRAYER STARTER

*Lord, I feel suffocated by sin's darkness sometimes. When I fall too deep, remind me of the light of Your Word that's always here to lead me out.*

## — 3 —

# THE VASTNESS OF GOD'S CREATION

*Thus the heavens and the earth were completed in all their vast array.*

GENESIS 2:1 NIV

Theodore Roosevelt often invited his friend William Beebe, an American naturalist and author, to spend time with him at his home in Cove Neck, New York. The two enjoyed spending time out on the lawn in the dark of night, and Roosevelt would point to the skies and recite, "That is the Spiral Galaxy in Andromeda. It is as large as our Milky Way. It is one of a hundred million galaxies. It consists of one hundred billion suns, each larger than our sun." Once he made that observation, Roosevelt would smile and say, "Now I think we are small enough! Let's go to bed."

If you've ever spent a night outdoors, away from the

city lights, you might have shared Roosevelt and Beebe's wonder. There's something about the beauty and vastness of the heavens—with its countless galaxies, stars, planets, and moons—that reminds us of how small we really are. . .but more importantly how big and awesome the Creator really is.

## FOR FURTHER THOUGHT

Studying the size of the cosmos can be terrifying. . .but it can also invoke a deep sense of praise. How might your worldview determine which emotion you feel?

How can the size of the universe be a powerful comfort for whenever you feel your problems are just too big for God to handle?

## PRAYER

*Glorious Father, thank You for filling the heavens with proof of Your incomprehensible power. . .and of Your inexhaustible love for Your tiniest creations.*

# — 4 —

# GREAT ACHIEVEMENTS

*But God made the earth by his power; he founded the world by his wisdom and stretched out the heavens by his understanding.*

JEREMIAH 10:12 NIV

Throughout history, the human race has engineered some truly amazing things. Machu Picchu, the "Lost City of the Incas," was built high in the environmentally hostile Peruvian Andes. The meticulous precision of the pyramids of Giza still defies explanation. And more recently, Mount Rushmore stands as one of the grandest stone carvings ever conceived.

While we observe these spectacles, words like *brilliant*, *incredible*, *fantastic*, or *magnificent* spring to mind. But interestingly, when God created our world and everything in it, He used a much simpler word to describe it all: *good.*

With that in mind, just imagine what God would consider

*genius.* In fact, we could never conceive such things—they're too far beyond our mental reach. Only our Creator can dream of that level of majesty. . .or produce it by simply speaking it into existence.

Our most remarkable achievements pale in comparison to those of our almighty God.

## FOR FURTHER THOUGHT

Humanity has built amazing things. . .using the things God has already created. How might nature itself be seen as a divine work of art?

What do you think is God's greatest masterpiece?

## PRAYER

*God, thank You for sharing with us Your appreciation for beauty. May the wonders of nature remind me of the wonders of Your power and grace.*

## — 5 —

# LORD OF THE TREES

*"And all the trees of the field shall know that I, the* L*ORD, have brought down the high tree, have exalted the low tree, have dried up the green tree, and have made the dry tree to flourish."*

EZEKIEL 17:24 SKJV

Over and over again, the Bible compares people to trees. For example, Psalm 1:1–3 describes the righteous person as a thriving, green tree planted by a river; and Ezekiel 31:3–7 pictures the king of Assyria and his kingdom as a lofty, proud cedar tree, towering over the other trees of the forest.

Trees provide a vivid illustration of the way God works in our lives: He can chop down tall trees in the height of their glory and exalt low, humble trees by replanting them in rich soil where they will grow. He is capable of drying up the green trees—the healthy and the wealthy—by taking away their water, and He can make a dry, dying tree suddenly flourish.

The variables that affect the trees are relatively simple compared to our complex lives—but God is sovereign and capable of doing exactly what He wishes.

## FOR FURTHER THOUGHT

A tree can only be truly strong if it's watered by God's love and grace. Which river are you planted beside today?

Healthy trees produce shade and fruit, attracting life and spreading nourishment. How are you benefiting others with the life-bringing fruit God provides?

## PRAYER

*Life-giving Lord, grow me into a mighty tree. I want alwqys to reach upward toward You, attracting others so that they may share in Your love.*

## — 6 —

# A GOD OF RESTORATION

*He makes me lie down in green pastures, he leads me beside quiet waters, he refreshes my soul.*

Psalm 23:2–3 niv

Ask several outdoorsmen what they like most about their time outside, and you're likely to receive several different answers. Some enjoy the peace, some the solitude, others the sense of being close to the Lord in a natural, God-created setting.

Alone in the wilderness, a person can learn things about God that could never be learned amidst the busyness and stress of everyday life. An individual can get to know God as the one who restores the mind, body, and spirit—and all through simple fellowship with the Holy Spirit.

When you're enjoying your favorite activity in a peaceful outdoor setting, remember that God wants to use that time to fellowship with you, teach you, and restore you as only He can.

## FOR FURTHER THOUGHT

God has designed every good thing in life so that it has the potential to lead us toward Him. How often do you use nature as an outlet to connect with God?

What have you learned about God while spending time in His creation?

## PRAYER

*Father, help me use every chance I get to strengthen my spiritual walk. May my love for the outdoors grow my love for You.*

# — 7 —

# WHEN STONES SPEAK

*And some of the Pharisees in the crowd said to him, "Teacher, rebuke your disciples." He answered, "I tell you, if these were silent, the very stones would cry out."*

LUKE 19:39–40 ESV

When you were young, did you ever skip stones across a pond or creek—maybe during a fishing trip or a hike with your dad? Those stones, the flatter the better, would bounce and skip and jump as many as a dozen times before gravity would finally win the battle and pull the rock underwater.

Stones are good for more than just skipping. They also provide fossil records that help us understand history. But they do even more than that. Stones have the ability to cry out when God's people fail to praise Him. The minute Jesus gave up His spirit on the cross, an earthquake split the rocks (Matthew 27:51). Man crucified Christ and the stones cried out for His glory.

The next time you take a walk, pick up a stone, look closely, and marvel over the fact that God can use such an object to glorify Himself.

## FOR FURTHER THOUGHT

Are you striving to live a life of continuous praise, or are you content to simply let the rocks do it for you?

All of creation—down to the tiniest pebble—screams the glory of God. How loudly are you willing to proclaim it today?

## PRAYER

*Lord God, Your splendor is found in everything, even in the rocks beneath my feet. Help me to recognize the sublimity in what others see as mundane.*

## — 8 —

# INHERITING THE GIFT

*There is but one God, the Father, from whom all things came and for whom we live.*

1 Corinthians 8:6 niv

Have you had the opportunity to paddle a canoe on a mountain lake? Ever caught sight of a hawk or eagle in flight? Have you visited one of the hundreds of natural wonders, large and small, around our nation? If so, did you contemplate the beauty of the scenery? God the Creator made it for each one of us.

Millions slog through life, oblivious to the panoramic slide show God has put on for them. Their busy lifestyles often shut them out from the beauty all around—and they miss the Creator who made it all.

If you're going through a hard time right now. . .if you're seeking answers to questions you're afraid to ask. . .if you're plagued with fatigue and disappointment, you're missing the secret. There's a gift right before your eyes, if you'll only look for it.

## FOR FURTHER THOUGHT

Do you regularly seek out God's gift of nature? If not, where might you begin trying today?

God designed the great outdoors to be therapeutic. How does the healing nature of His creation point us toward His love for us?

## PRAYER

*God, thank You for putting me in a world brimming with beauty, infusing light into even my darkest hours. May I always be attentive to this gift.*

## — 9 —

# LISTEN TO THE SILENCE

*Then Jesus said, "Whoever has ears to hear, let them hear."*

MARK 4:9 NIV

On a still, winter night in the country, the silence might surprise you. The almost complete lack of noise somehow clears the mind and points us to deeper thoughts.

Most of us rarely experience this kind of quiet. Our minds are accustomed to a false silence—a steady din of distant traffic, heating systems, and unintelligible chatter that we subconsciously tune out.

Sadly, it's easy to do the same thing in our Christian life. We "tune out" the little sins that creep into our day, and we think we're doing all right. But when we're truly silent before God, those little sins scream like chain saws cutting through the still winter air—shocking us out of our complacency and compelling us to act.

Find some real, soul-refreshing silence. Stop tuning out distractions—instead, run far away from them, listening intently for God's voice to fill the void they left behind. Hear His instructions, and become more and more the child He wants you to be.

## FOR FURTHER THOUGHT

Which scene does your soul resemble on most days: a quiet, peaceful lake or a raging sea? Why?

When is the last time you did some soul-searching, seeking out the solitude of nature to examine your relationship with God?

## PRAYER

*God, my sins pollute the peace of my soul. Give me the stillness of mind to single out these transgressions and put an end to them today.*

## — 10 —

# BEYOND OUR FURTHEST LIMITS

*The eyes of the* Lord *are in every place,*
*watching the evil and the good.*
Proverbs 15:3 SKJV

In 1953 Edmund Hillary and Tenzing Norgay became the first people to set foot on the summit of Mount Everest. Within minutes of reaching this hitherto undisturbed corner of the earth, Hillary dug a hole in the snow and buried a cross there. Given the summit's perpetual deep freeze, the cross might still be there more than half a century later.

One thing is sure: before these men reached that summit, before the cross was buried there, God was already there. After all, He made the place!

When we set out on organized expeditions or personal explorations, we mustn't feel the need to colonize nature with God's glory. He's already there, waiting for us to discover Him with eyes of faith.

## FOR FURTHER THOUGHT

What are some of the places in which you've experienced God most powerfully? Were you seeking the revelation, or did it come by surprise?

How might knowing that God is present in every inch of His creation increase our desire to explore it?

Why is mankind's quest to control nature often inferior to the desire to learn from it?

## PRAYER

*Lord, thank You for being everywhere. The further into the wilderness I travel, the deeper I feel Your presence.*

## 11

# THE AWESOME AUROCHS

*"Will the wild ox consent to serve you? Will it stay by your manger at night? Can you hold it to the furrow with a harness? Will it till the valleys behind you? Will you rely on it for its great strength? Will you leave your heavy work to it?"*

JOB 39:9–11 NIV

The wild ox—the aurochs—was the ancestor of modern cattle but was far larger, stronger, and more ferocious than bred-down domestic oxen. Aurochs bulls weighed over twenty-two hundred pounds, and as Julius Caesar wrote, "Their strength and speed are extraordinary; they spare neither man nor wild beast." The ancients could only dream of harnessing the power of such creatures.

Aurochs once roamed free throughout Europe and the Middle East. Hunting them was considered such a test of courage and manhood that, over the millennia, they were driven to the point of extinction. The last wild ox died in Poland in 1627.

In today's utilitarian, results-oriented world, we try to find a practical use for everything, some purpose to justify its existence—but some things just *are*. Some wild creatures exist simply to cause us to consider the power and majesty of the God who created them.

## FOR FURTHER THOUGHT

God has established the natural order to serve His purpose, not to be exploited for our selfishness. How appreciative are you of the natural beauty you encounter?

What might the story of the aurochs teach us about our role as caretakers of God's creation?

## PRAYER

*God, thank You for the pristine beauty of Your creation. May I never grow so cynical as to exploit it for ugly, prideful reasons.*

# — 12 —

# DETAILS OF CREATION

*For you created my inmost being; you knit me together in my mother's womb. I praise you because I am fearfully and wonderfully made; your works are wonderful, I know that full well.*

PSALM 139:13–14 NIV

Macrophotography dramatically enlarges the smallest details of a flower, a butterfly, a bee, or even a spider in a web. Such scenic work is a wonderful way to inspect the intricate workmanship of God's creation.

Though we as human beings were engineered with the same kind of care and detail, depression and low self-esteem often blind us to the value we have in God's eyes. But just like the intricacies of a monarch butterfly, an Oriental lily, or a simple rose point to God's creativity, the painstaking detail found in our bodies, minds, and personalities should bring us to an admiration of His handiwork.

Each of us is "fearfully and wonderfully made" by the great Creator of the universe. Who knows how much time He spent designing each one of us before the foundation of the world? His thoughts toward us outnumber the grains of sand.

## FOR FURTHER THOUGHT

All of us have unique traits we're embarrassed to reveal to others. How can the child of God find evidence of God's design in what some may consider a flaw?

God wants us to use all of our being to bring glory to Him. How are you employing your passions, hopes, and skills to advance His kingdom?

## PRAYER

*Lord, if You spent all that time designing a single leaf, I know You worked even harder making me. Help me discover the potential You've placed within me.*

## — 13 —

# POLE, POLE

*The fastest runner doesn't always win the race, and the strongest warrior doesn't always win the battle.*

ECCLESIASTES 9:11 NLT

Mount Kilimanjaro rises 19,340 feet above the African plain, attracting many an adventurer eager to reach Africa's highest peak.

"Kili" may be climbed without technical skills, but the guides constantly remind the climbers, "*Pole, pole. . .*" *Pole* means "slow" in Swahili. The guides know that those who start out hiking fast will later be found by the side of the trail gasping for breath in the thin air. Those who succeed in reaching the summit of the world's highest freestanding mountain are those who have learned the secret of just putting one foot in front of the other, thousands and thousands of times in succession.

Our daily life is much like Kilimanjaro. God doesn't need us to be bottle rockets, zipping by fast, making a loud pop, and quickly fading away. Instead, He wants long-term faithfulness and growth. Truly rising in Christian maturity requires a consistent dedication to weathering life's peaks and valleys.

## FOR FURTHER THOUGHT

How does Mount Kilimanjaro resemble the mountains that often arise in the life of a Christian?

Why do you think God gives us these mountains as opposed to letting us sprint freely across flat terrain?

## PRAYER

*Lord, Maker of the hills, imbue me with consistent willpower, not just brief flashes of strength. In my journey toward You, I'm determined to reach the top.*

## — 14 —

# OUR GOD IS UNIQUE

*There is no one holy like the* Lord, *for there is no one besides You, nor is there any rock like our God.*

1 Samuel 2:2 skjv

At nearly six miles in circumference, Australia's Uluru is probably the largest rock in the world.

But there's something else that sets Uluru, also known as Ayers Rock, apart: its apparently shifting color scheme. Depending on the sunlight and weather, it can change from silvery-gray to brown to orange to red. Known by geologists as an *inselberg*, or "island mountain," local Aborigines see the massive rock as sacred.

The Bible describes our God as a sacred "rock." There is no other God like Him. His many names and titles—including Abba Father, Bridegroom, Friend, High Priest, I Am, King of Kings, Mediator, Only Begotten Son, Redeemer, Savior, and Strength—indicate the incredible breadth of

His personality and power.

Unique landmarks are interesting—but our God is truly special. Whatever trouble, sorrow, or frustration we're experiencing, our God is big enough to cover them all. That's what makes our Rock so unique and valuable!

## FOR FURTHER THOUGHT

What attributes of God strike you as the most unique?

How do the various items in nature—from large rocks to the frailest of insects—reflect different aspects of God's character?

How have you seen God's unique qualities at play in your own life?

## PRAYER

*Father, thank You for giving us so many reasons to worship You. Your complexity is infinite, always revealing itself in new and exciting ways.*

## — 15 —

# FEAR NOT—GOD KNOWS

*"Are not two sparrows sold for a penny? And not one of them will fall to the ground apart from your Father. . . . Fear not, therefore; you are of more value than many sparrows."*

MATTHEW 10:29, 31 ESV

Woodland birds don't care who's watching, as long as the observer remains silent. Their pursuit of food and other necessities is patient and unhurried, free from pride or worry about success. They just stick to the job until they have what they need.

It can be amusing to see a sparrow stop hopping along a rotten log to flip a maple leaf onto the ground. When it repeats the action with another leaf, we begin to give the bird a little more credit: it seems to be making decisions.

God knows what's going on in that bird brain—and He knows what's going on in our lives. We don't need to worry about our future meals or the state of the economy. God knows our needs, and He's promised to supply.

He counts us more valuable than many sparrows.

## FOR FURTHER THOUGHT

God provides for all His creation—from the lumbering elephant down to the tiniest brainless bacterium. How does the cycle of life illustrate God's attention to detail?

How might you go about developing a "natural" attitude toward the future—concerned only with your present needs and trusting God for the rest?

## PRAYER

*Father, overthinking can be a curse, when I try to reach beyond what I'm created to understand. Teach me to fearlessly accept Your mysteries.*

## — 16 —

# BUT CAN YOU FLY?

*"The wings of the ostrich flap joyfully,*
*though they cannot compare with the*
*wings and feathers of the stork."*
Job 39:13 NIV

Four thousand years ago, ostriches flourished in the land of Uz, east of Canaan, on the fringes of the Arabian Desert. Later, wealthy Arabs hunted ostriches for food and for sport. The introduction of motor vehicles and firearms in the early twentieth century spelled the birds' demise, and the last Arabian ostrich died in Jordan in 1966.

Flocks of black storks, by contrast, still migrate annually over the Middle East, flying thousands of miles from Europe to Africa. The stork is a significantly sized bird, and while not as large as the ostrich, it has one distinct advantage: the ostrich merely waves its wings proudly as it runs, but the stork can actually fly.

Many of us might choose to be a powerful heavyweight like an ostrich, with the speed and power to outrun hounds and horses and arrows. But ostriches can't escape big guns. When a trouble too fast to outrun comes along, it's better to be a lightweight stork that can spread its wings and rise into the heavens for refuge.

## FOR FURTHER THOUGHT

What are some problems in your life that you've tried (and failed) to run away from? How might things have been different if you'd faced them head on?

How can a Christian rise above life's challenges? What spiritual skills must we hone to more closely resemble the stork?

## PRAYER

*Lord, give me the strength and wisdom to fly to You for refuge. You've given me the wings of Your Spirit—help me use them.*

## — 17 —

# THE BLACK WIDOW

*The fear of the* Lord *is the beginning of wisdom; all those who practice it have a good understanding. His praise endures forever!*

Psalm 111:10 esv

The most venomous spider in North America is the black widow. It generally lives in the warmer, southern states, hiding in woodpiles, garages, and other dark places. Its venom is said to be fifteen times more poisonous than a rattlesnake's and works by disrupting the central nervous system.

Those bites are relatively rare, though: the spiders prefer to hide or run away rather than tangle with a person. If you leave them alone, they'll likely never bother you. Black widows really give us little to fear but much to respect.

This is the kind of fear today's verse speaks of. The fear of the Lord is all about respect and reverence. We need not be frightened of Him—He loves us! But the respectful reverence we give God in all things is the basis of our whole relationship with Him.

## FOR FURTHER THOUGHT

How do some Christians fall short of today's verse? How do others take it to an unhealthy extreme?

What are some other natural phenomena that inspire a reverent type of fear? How might some of these be even more suitable illustrations for the fear we should show toward God?

## PRAYER

*Thank You, God, for being a source of comfort for me. May my fear of You always be tempered with my appreciation for Your love—and vice versa.*

## — 18 —

# THE STOREHOUSE OF SNOW

*"Have you entered the storehouses of the snow or seen the storehouses of the hail, which I reserve for times of trouble, for days of war and battle?"*

JOB 38:22–23 NIV

One of the most beautiful sights of nature is a winter snowfall.

Snow has a distinct cleansing effect as it covers everything in a blanket of white. The sight of those big, fluffy flakes floating down like feathers from heaven is calming—as is the thick powder's sound-deadening effect. A good snowfall muffles the noise of the surrounding world, somehow slowing the pace of our hurry-up society.

But then comes the fun. Sleds, snowmobiles, forts, snowmen, and snowballs appear. The world becomes a different place after a good snowfall.

Yes, a "storehouse of snow" is truly one of God's most

amazing gifts—and an awesome proof of His unbridled creativity.

## FOR FURTHER THOUGHT

Many people overlook the snow's beauty, focusing instead on the inconvenience it brings. What might a person's reaction to snow reveal about his outlook on life?

It's said that no two snowflakes are identical. How does this mind-boggling degree of variety further prove God's meticulous care for His creation?

## PRAYER

*Father, snow is common enough to be taken for granted. . .but rare enough to be fully appreciated by those with spiritual eyes. Thank You for this gift.*

## — 19 —

# WHEN WINTER ENDS

*See! The winter is past; the rains are over and gone. Flowers appear on the earth; the season of singing has come, the cooing of doves is heard in our land.*

Song of Solomon 2:11–12 niv

In ancient times, just like today, winter was a hard time—a season to be endured. Of course, winter in Israel didn't usually feature the subzero temperatures and heavy snows that North America experiences.

Still, spring was a time of rejoicing. The cold winter rains had passed, and signs of life were appearing. Flowers began to bud. Birds began mating. The low, contented cooing of doves could be heard. It was a happy time, "the season of singing."

Like it or not, all of us go through winter seasons, times of prolonged sorrow or moments of seemingly insufferable despair. But God's promise remains true: "Weeping may stay for the night, but rejoicing comes in the morning" (Psalm 30:5 NIV).

Winter will always give way to spring. Just don't give up hope!

## FOR FURTHER THOUGHT

How does the continuous cycling of the seasons symbolize the patterns of our lives?

What are some ways people prepare for winter? How can the Christian prepare for the cold season that may be around the corner?

## PRAYER

*Lord, I hate going through spiritual winter. . .but I know it's often necessary. Keep me warm with the faith-fueled fire of Your promises.*

## — 20 —

# HOPE OF THE RESURRECTION

*"As the water of a lake dries up or a riverbed becomes parched and dry, so he lies down and does not rise; till the heavens are no more, people will not awake or be roused from their sleep."*

JOB 14:11–12 NIV

In the western Arabian Desert bordering Uz, there are scores of landlocked rivers with no outlet to the oceans. Instead, brief rainstorms cause them to surge into myriad shallow depressions, forming inland seas. But the water doesn't last. The land bakes like an oven in the desert heat, leaving behind bone-dry wadis and large, cracked salt pans.

Job noted that man's life was like these short-lived wadis and seas. Some might read this desolate imagery and conclude that we live, we die, and that's it. But upon closer inspection, this verse is brimming with hope: one day, the heavens and the earth will indeed pass away. . .bringing with it a restoration of all things—a final, triumphant resurrection.

As Job said in the next verses: "If someone dies, will they live again? All the days of my hard service I will wait for my renewal to come" (verse 14 NIV). We, too, wait to be renewed.

## FOR FURTHER THOUGHT

Have you ever had a "dried-up lakebed" season in your life? How do such seasons—and the relief that comes afterward—prepare us for God's ultimate renewal that awaits us?

Why is the historical fact of Jesus' resurrection so important to our own lives and hopes today?

## PRAYER

*God, I'm a thirsty soul in a dry, dusty world. I know nothing in this life will ever satisfy me—so I eagerly desire renewal by Your living water.*

## — 21 —

# THE GRAND CANYON(S)

*Follow God's example, therefore,*
*as dearly loved children.*
EPHESIANS 5:1 NIV

Whether you've been there or not, you're probably familiar with the Grand Canyon, the massive Arizona gorge carved out by the Colorado River. It is one of the United States' oldest national parks.

But other locales claim the "Grand Canyon" name as well. There's "the Grand Canyon of Pennsylvania"—Pine Creek Gorge in the north central section of the Keystone State—and at least two places that bill themselves as "the Grand Canyon of the East": Letchworth State Park near Perry, New York, and the New River Gorge National Park near Fayetteville, West Virginia.

If imitation is the sincerest form of flattery, the real Grand Canyon should be pleased—just as God is pleased when we imitate Him.

How can we imitate God? Read the verses following Ephesians 5:1 for a few ideas: "Walk in the way of love, just as Christ loved us and gave himself up for us as a fragrant offering and sacrifice to God. But among you there must not be even a hint of sexual immorality, or of any kind of impurity, or of greed, because these are improper for God's holy people" (Ephesians 5:2–3 NIV).

## FOR FURTHER THOUGHT

Just as none of these locations can fully mimic the Grand Canyon's splendor, we can never replicate God's righteousness. Yet He still wants us to try. Why?

How well would you say you're imitating God?

## PRAYER

*Almighty God, my ultimate goal is Your holiness. I know I'll never reach it in this life, but I want to get as close as possible.*

## — 22 —

# THE COLORFUL MACAW

*"Blessed are those who are persecuted because of righteousness, for theirs is the kingdom of heaven. Blessed are you when people insult you, persecute you and falsely say all kinds of evil against you because of me."*

MATTHEW 5:10–11 NIV

The macaw is a beautiful bird—its red, blue, yellow, white, or green feathers make it one of the most colorful creatures in the world. There's no mistaking this amazing avian, even from far away.

The very thing that makes the macaw such a beautiful bird, however, also makes it an easy target for predators. Killers like large cats, other birds, and even human beings have a fairly easy time stalking these birds. It's tough to hide when wearing such vivid colors!

As Christians, we may often feel like easy targets too.

The love of Jesus that shows through our lives is frequently the very thing that attracts trouble. But Jesus understands that, and He assures us in His Word that He'll accompany us all the way to heaven.

Don't be afraid to show your true colors. The God who created you for His glory will see you through, also for His glory.

## FOR FURTHER THOUGHT

Many Christians try adapting their faith to the world. What are the dangers in this pursuit?

How might dwelling on Jesus' ultimate sacrifice lessen your feelings of awkwardness when you're singled out for your faith?

## PRAYER

*Holy God, in a world as broken as this, why would I try blending in? Strengthen me to boldly show the beautiful colors of Your love.*

## — 23 —

# EVERYTHING HAS A PURPOSE

*There is one glory of the sun, and another glory of the moon, and another glory of the stars; for star differs from star in glory.*

1 Corinthians 15:41 ESV

People who believe the earth came into being by chance can't fathom a God in heaven who spoke everything into existence and now sustains it. But the redeemed know better. We understand that God not only created everything but keeps it in smooth running order. And everything He does has a purpose.

The sun has one kind of glory and the moon another. Individual stars have yet a different glory. Humans don't even know how many stars exist—but God knows the exact number, since He created each one uniquely.

Many people go through life trying to make sense of a supposedly random universe. But we can rest in the knowledge that God isn't fretting or trying to figure things out. He knew and knows exactly what's it all means.

## FOR FURTHER THOUGHT

Life on earth requires a host of incredibly fine-tuned conditions to exist. How does knowing this impact your reliance on God's provision in your life?

Assuming that humanity will never know every detail about the universe, how does this raise your appreciation of God's complete knowledge?

## PRAYER

*All-knowing God, Your understanding is infinite—greater even than the universe You've created. Teach me to rely on Your unsurpassable wisdom.*

## — 24 —

# IN THE DARK OF NIGHT

*"He alone stretches out the heavens and treads on the waves of the sea. He is the Maker of the Bear and Orion, the Pleiades and the constellations of the south."*

JOB 9:8–9 NIV

Those of us who live in cities—even in much smaller towns—often miss one of the greatest testimonies of God's creative power. That's because "light pollution" obscures the breath-taking view of the countless stars He hung in the heavens.

But out in the country, far from streetlights, illuminated billboards, and twenty-four-hour gas stations, those stars have a chance to speak a great truth to our souls. Even Job, separated from us by millennia, looked at these same stars and drew the same conclusion—God made it all.

Take every chance you get to enjoy a truly dark night. Let the Bear, Orion, the Pleiades, and the thousands of other stars visible to the naked eye point you to the God who alone stretched out the heavens.

## FOR FURTHER THOUGHT

Beyond what the naked eye can see, it's estimated that roughly two hundred billion trillion stars exist in the universe. How does learning more about creation increase our appreciation of God's power?

What are some ways you can escape the world's spiritual "light pollution" in order to more fully appreciate the mysteries of God?

## PRAYER

*Lord, whenever I look at the stars, I feel so small—and I recognize how big You are. Help me to remember that truth when I need Your help.*

# — 25 —

# THE CATHEDRAL OF THE WORLD

*Happy is he who has the God of Jacob for his help, whose hope is in the LORD his God, who made heaven and earth, the sea, and all that is in it, who keeps truth forever.*

PSALM 146:5–6 SKJV

The Cathedral of the Pines is in the New Hampshire countryside. Envisaged as a "cathedral without walls," this park area was set up as a permanent memorial to those who gave their lives for this country. Now it's a place of retreat and contemplation, and the sense of peace it offers makes it a popular venue for weddings.

But there's a deeper truth implicit in the very name of the place. Humans have built some impressive cathedrals over the centuries. Many will take your breath away, but none of them will be as intricately wonderful as a single tree.

We like to have special places to worship—we feel our

God deserves no less. Well, look outside. He already created the grandest, most spectacular place of worship for us. The Cathedral of the Pines is just a fraction of its grandeur.

## FOR FURTHER THOUGHT

Have you ever talked with God in the forest, on a lake, or on a hiking trail? How is this experience somewhat different than a traditional prayer in a church setting?

When's the last time you thanked God for giving you the opportunity to witness such impressive proofs of His strength?

## PRAYER

*Lord Jesus, the universe is Your house of worship. May I never fail to fall reverently before You whenever I see reminders of Your glory.*

# — 26 —

# THE MIND'S EYE

*"I am the good shepherd; I know my sheep and my sheep know me."*
JOHN 10:14 NIV

Ever "see something" in the clouds—an elephant, a boat, Abraham Lincoln's profile?

That's because our eyes recognize patterns. In a huge crowd of people, we can recognize the one person we know because our mind remembers the pattern and spatial relationships of a face. And if a natural object—like a cloud—looks enough like this pattern, our mind's eye will fill in the blanks and cause us to "see" something that isn't there.

The brain's memory system truly is amazing, but think of this: God recognizes *every* person who's ever lived. Not only does He know us, He's concerned about us in a very personal way. He understands our struggles and celebrates our joys.

God knows us so well that He even knows how many hairs we have. Nobody on earth knows so much about another person, no matter how much he might love that person.

How much God cares for us individually is beyond the reach of our imagination.

## FOR FURTHER THOUGHT

God created our minds to be dim but beautiful reflections of His own. How might your feelings of love for other people point toward the degree of love God has for you?

Given the fact that God cares enough to know you personally, how hard are you striving to know Him?

## PRAYER

*Lord, thank You for knowing me better than I know myself. Even when I'm confused and conflicted, I can entrust myself to You.*

## — 27 —

# SEEN FROM ABOVE

*He has made everything beautiful in its time. He has also set eternity in the human heart; yet no one can fathom what God has done from beginning to end.*

ECCLESIASTES 3:11 NIV

Butterflies have a spectacular array of colorful patterns decorating their wings—on the top sides! But the undersides of their wings are seldom so striking. Often, the patterns and colors are pale imitations; sometimes, they are completely black.

Which side does the butterfly see? Does a butterfly on a stalk of grass see itself as we see it, looking down from above? Or does it see the dull, black side? Would it even understand our concept of beauty?

From time to time, we might give in to self-doubt and despair, seeing only the darker sides of our personalities. But the little butterfly is a constant reminder that no matter what we might think of ourselves, there is more to us. We are all attractive and desirable to the God who sees us from above.

## FOR FURTHER THOUGHT

How does knowing that God sees the good side of you provide comfort when all you can see is bad?

Why does God allow human beings to struggle with a good and bad side? How can we come to terms with this aspect of our human existence?

## PRAYER

*Father, thank You for the bright side—the beauty that's always there, even when I can't see it. Teach me to look for Your signature in everything.*

## — 28 —

# THE WAVES OBEY GOD

*You rule the raging of the sea;*
*when its waves rise, you still them.*
PSALM 89:9 ESV

Insurance companies write provisions into their policies concerning "acts of God"—uncontrollable weather-related damage to personal property.

We humans inherently know that weather is beyond our control. But have we considered that it's completely within God's power? He can command sea waves to rise and then be calm again.

Though He's not obligated to explain His reasoning, God has a purpose in everything He does. Perhaps His control over the sea is designed to make us marvel at His power. From our limited human perspective, ocean waves seem like chaos. But God created them to obey Him—and they do that willingly. Each wave that crashes onto the shoreline testifies to God's power.

## FOR FURTHER THOUGHT

How does knowing that God has charted the paths of every seemingly random ocean wave give us more faith in His control over our lives?

Waves erode things, sometimes quickly but usually over long periods. How might God be using the waves in your life to erode parts of you that need to change?

## PRAYER

*Lord, You're the Master of the sea, even the sea that's raging all around me now. I trust that each wave will serve Your ultimate purpose.*

# — 29 —

# HEARING GOD IN THE QUIET

*After the fire came a gentle whisper. When Elijah heard it, he pulled his cloak over his face and went out and stood at the mouth of the cave.*

1 Kings 19:12–13 NIV

It's easy sometimes to hear the spectacular sounds of nature and think of the magnificent power of God. The ear-jolting clap of thunder, the roaring of a waterfall, the relentless howl of a strong wind rushing through the trees—all these things remind us of the awesome power of God.

The Bible includes many accounts of God talking to mankind through the spectacular. He talked to Moses through a burning bush and to Job through a whirlwind. But when the deeply discouraged prophet Elijah wanted to hear from God, he had to listen *past* some of nature's most impressive displays—a powerful wind, an earthquake, and then a fire.

It's an awesome thought to realize that God can speak

to us in any way He wants. But it's also comforting to know that when we long for strength and encouragement, all we need to do is listen for His gentle voice above the noise.

## FOR FURTHER THOUGHT

How is God's power revealed in the gentle croaking of a frog just the same as it is in the raging of a tornado?

How can followers of God train themselves to look beyond the superficial crashing and roaring of life and into the peace that lies at the heart of it all?

## PRAYER

*Father God, Your voice is sometimes hard to hear amid the frightening sounds all around me. Give me clarity of mind so that I can discern Your whisper.*

## — 30 —

# COUNTING THE STARS

*And [God] brought [Abram] outside and said, "Look toward heaven, and number the stars, if you are able to number them." Then he said to him, "So shall your offspring be."*

GENESIS 15:5 ESV

In 2003, a group of Australian astronomers conducted a study using two of the world's most powerful telescopes in an attempt to number the stars. They found some ten thousand galaxies and estimated that there are approximately seventy thousand million million million (or seventy sextillion) stars. The astronomers said this number was limited by the range of modern telescopes and that, in reality, the actual number of stars "could be infinite."

Indeed, since that day, we've discovered countless more, bringing the number to somewhere near two trillion galaxies, each containing dozens of billions of stars.

Step outside your house tonight and look up into the sky.

Try to number the stars you can see, keeping in mind that you have only a microscopic view of the big picture. Once you're overwhelmed by the task—as Abram surely was—whisper a prayer of thanks to God for His willingness to make, and ability to keep, His promise to Abram and his descendants. Because through that promise, *you* found salvation.

## FOR FURTHER THOUGHT

Abram had no way of knowing how many stars existed. How might this fact cause us to reevaluate our assumptions about God's plans for us?

God's promises are often too big to comprehend at the time. How can the act of studying nature expand our minds to better grasp the limitless nature of His power?

## PRAYER

*Lord, Maker of the stars, thank You for promising blessings that exceed the stars in number. I'll never tire of Your infinite goodness.*

## — 31 —

# WHICH WAY THEN?

*And when his time of service was ended, he went to his home.*
LUKE 1:23 ESV

Each year, salmon, which have spent most of their life at sea, begin an amazing journey. Somehow, they return to the river where they first met the sea and begin to swim upstream.

Some salmon have been known to travel up to a thousand miles against the current, rising thousands of feet above sea level. Along the way they have to get past fishermen, bears, even waterfalls. Many never make it, but they all try. Why? They're driven by a powerful urge to get home before they spawn and die.

Similarly, humans are compelled by God's Spirit to "come home" to the Creator who made them. Sadly, unlike the fish, many people reason their way out of His love and mercy, ending up even worse off than the salmon that perish on the journey.

Today, let's make two commitments: to be sure we're personally following God's call to come home, and to invite others around us to come along.

## FOR FURTHER THOUGHT

The main difference between an animal and a human is the fact that humans have free will. Why do you think God gave us this wonderful, dangerous gift?

Are you resisting the instinctual homeward call of God's Spirit, or are you letting it drive you to a brighter future? Why?

## PRAYER

*Lord, I want to be like the salmon—so focused on the beacon You've placed in my heart that nothing else matters. May I be wholly obedient today.*

## — 32 —

# LORD OF THE STONE

*Now on the first day of the week Mary Magdalene came to the tomb early, while it was still dark, and saw that the stone had been taken away from the tomb.*

JOHN 20:1 ESV

Many of us who love the outdoors are accustomed to waking before the sun rises. The solitude and peacefulness to be found outside are well worth the early hour. We go forth seeking an encounter with God, knowing He'll show up.

When Mary Magdalene rose early to visit Jesus' tomb, she had no such expectations. She was simply zealous in her love for Christ and wanted to show her respects. So imagine her surprise when she saw that the stone door of the tomb had been rolled away. Mary first wept, thinking Jesus' body had been stolen—but quickly learned from angels that Jesus had risen from the dead. Soon, she was face to face with her Lord, who had conquered the tomb, the stone door, and death itself.

As you seek God in the wilderness, go with the knowledge that He will meet you there.

## FOR FURTHER THOUGHT

Have you ever been deeply rewarded by choosing to seek God at an early hour?

While you were out in nature, has God ever surprised you by revealing more of His truth than you had sought?

In what ways can you see echoes of the story of redemption within the natural world?

## PRAYER

*Lord, every cave reminds me of the empty tomb; every stone, of the stone You rolled away; every sign of death or decay, of Your triumphant resurrection.*

# — 33 —

# "THE GRUNION ARE RUNNING!"

*God saw all that he had made,*
*and it was very good.*
GENESIS 1:31 NIV

Some Californians live for one announcement: "The grunion are running!" No, it's not a new marathon; it's a unique creation event occurring over a brief period on certain southern beaches.

Don't tell any true believer that the unique silver fish called a *grunion* is a happenstance of nature. No! It's just one "oddity" in God's grand design that He called "very good."

For reasons known only to their Creator, the slippery little silver fish beach themselves as "couples" by the thousands. With a little dance, eggs are buried in the sand and fertilized. Later, the baby grunion evade predators on their way to the sea from whence their parents came.

Like the swallows that return to Capistrano every year,

each of these seven-inch fish has a God-given compass that points toward home—the beach on which they were born.

## FOR FURTHER THOUGHT

The animal kingdom is filled with odd, inexplicable instincts and rituals that cry out for a brilliant Maker. What are some other examples you can think of?

Grunion don't question the instincts that draw them toward the beach—they just follow. How can Christians learn from the grunion?

Where is the God-given longing in your heart taking you?

## PRAYER

*Almighty God, teach me to be like the grunion—eager to follow Your instructions, no matter how odd they may seem. May I never resist Your spiritual instincts.*

## — 34 —

# THE MASTER'S VOICE

*"Instead of the thorn, the fir tree shall come up, and instead of the briar, the myrtle tree shall come up. And it shall be to the* Lord *for a name, for an everlasting sign that shall not be cut off."*

Isaiah 55:13 SKJV

How does a tree know how high it's supposed to grow? What makes the leaves appear, change colors, and fall off at the same time? Why do those leaves turn upward just before a storm?

When God spoke the world into existence, He placed inside each living thing a knowledge of its perfect purpose. His will for each life—whether tree, bush, animal, or person—is carefully embedded within, though we human beings often rebel against it.

The next time you walk among trees, think about the God who gave each one its purpose. Take a moment to contemplate the complexity of creation. Each of those trees, every rock, all the blades of grass know their Creator. They recognize Him when He speaks their name across the universe.

Will we listen as He speaks to us today?

## FOR FURTHER THOUGHT

One famous scientist has referred to the DNA inside all living things as the "language of God." What are some other ways God communicates with His creation?

Have you ever thought that God is using the things that happen in your life to actualize your potential—just like the sunshine and rain work together to pull a tree out from a seed?

## PRAYER

*Lord, the information—the written destinies—stored inside each creature reminds me of the destiny You've mapped out for me. Help me pursue that calling each day.*

# — 35 —

# CREATOR AND SUSTAINER

*"I say to you, unless a grain of wheat falls into the ground and dies, it remains alone. But if it dies, it brings forth much fruit."*
JOHN 12:24 SKJV

The spectacle of nature is as beautiful as it is predictable. Each year, the cycle of birth, life, and death begins, ends, and soon begins again.

Consider, for example, the stone fly. Fly fishermen know that each spring, the stone fly nymph crawls onto dry land, sheds its skin, mates. . .and then deposits its eggs back into the river and dies. The process ensures another generation of stone flies, but it also provides food for the birds and fish that live near the river—not to mention a great season of fly-fishing!

These things don't happen by chance. The same God who set all things in motion works year-round to sustain them, to bring them back to their proper places at the proper time.

If God cares that much for stone flies, think how much He cares for you.

## FOR FURTHER THOUGHT

How does the cycle of life—which, here on earth, inevitably involves death—point us to our greater hope in eternity?

What "deaths" have you experienced lately? What rebirths? Are you willing to let God create purpose from both the joy and the pain?

## PRAYER

*Father, let the losses that I feel in my soul only serve to fertilize the soil of hope. Thank You for bringing life from death.*

## — 36 —

# THE MASTER ARTIST

*"You alone are the* Lord. *You made the heavens, even the highest heavens, and all their starry host, the earth and all that is on it, the seas and all that is in them. You give life to everything, and the multitudes of heaven worship you."*

Nehemiah 9:6 niv

Driving through the Ozark hills south toward the Boston Mountains can be an awe-inspiring trip. At times, the angle of the highway is such that you feel you might drive right into the heavens. The richness of the blue sky, the brilliance of the sun, the bulk of the mountains, and the beauty of the scenery provide a breathtaking panorama, better than any painting you've ever seen in a museum.

God, the master artist, has unveiled a work that gives a slight glimpse into the majesty of His entire creation. When you think of this planet traveling 67,000 miles an hour around a sun 93 million miles away—all of it traveling some 500,000 miles an hour around one of billions of galaxies—how can that be anything other than a spiritual experience?

## FOR FURTHER THOUGHT

How is "losing yourself" in a natural landscape similar to losing yourself within God's glory? How might one be a form of the other?

When is the last time you were in awe over a natural scene? What did you do in that moment?

## PRAYER

*Father God, You're the greatest artist of all, and Your masterpieces are too numerous to count. Thank You for allowing me to witness Your brilliance.*

## — 37 —

# SMALL CREATIONS

*I went down to the grove of nut trees to look at the new growth in the valley, to see if the vines had budded or the pomegranates were in bloom.*

Song of Solomon 6:11 NIV

People with grapevines in their backyards understand the feeling of happy anticipation that Solomon describes in this verse. But, we might ask, why would the ruler of an empire stretching from Egypt to the Euphrates have been excited by the sight of mere grapes beginning to bud?

For the same reason that we today, busy as we are with high-level, pressing projects and important accomplishments, enjoy seeing the first carrots appear in our garden. Not only are they a promise of good things to come, we find relaxation and joy just looking at them.

The beloved of Solomon's love story exclaimed, "Let us go *early* to the vineyards to see if the vines have budded"

(Song of Solomon 7:12 NIV, emphasis added). God's small creations are good for your soul.

## FOR FURTHER THOUGHT

The more advanced humanity becomes, the more complex and worrisome our schedules get. How often do you take breaks to appreciate life's simple pleasures?

Do you believe God designed nature to be therapeutic? How?

## PRAYER

*Lord, open my eyes to the tiny wonders that populate my world. Reveal to me the subtle but all-encompassing signs of Your glory.*

## — 38 —

# THE WAY OF AN EAGLE

*[The* Lord *was] like an eagle that stirs up its nest and hovers over its young, that spreads its wings to catch them and carries them aloft.*

Deuteronomy 32:11 niv

For the past two centuries, the eagle has been the national bird and symbol of the United States. But for millennia, mankind has admired the eagle as an icon of unfettered freedom and fierceness in battle. The biblical proverb writer Agur said that one of the most awe-inspiring things he could think of was "how an eagle glides through the sky" (Proverbs 30:19 nlt).

Though it is the epitome of power and independence of spirit, there is something even more poignant and wonderful about an eagle—how fiercely protective it is of its young. And that is how God is toward those who love and obey Him.

God hovered over the Israelites in the wilderness,

sheltered them, and led them on to the promised land. That same God lives today and hovers over you, protecting you when you stay in the shadow of His wings.

And when you stumble, God is there to lift you back up with those same wings.

## FOR FURTHER THOUGHT

Can you think of a time when God covered you like an eagle? How was your soul strengthened during this trying period?

How should the fact that God created the eagle give us comfort when it comes to our safety? How much more powerful is God in comparison with this mighty bird?

## PRAYER

*Lord, thank You for being a shadow of rest for me when I needed it the most. I trust in You more than any protection on earth.*

## — 39 —

# WHEN THE WIND BLOWS. . .

*For You have been a strength to the poor, a strength to the needy in his distress, a refuge from the storm, a shadow from the heat, when the blast of the terrifying ones is as a storm against the wall.*

Isaiah 25:4 SKJV

The Israelites were accustomed to the east wind that blew in from the Arabian Desert, and they were always prepared for the especially hot and destructive gale that came on occasion.

When a windstorm broke in all its fury, hissing with dust and sand, Israelites scrambled to their houses. There, they listened to the blast of the wind against their walls and thanked God for safety. Isaiah praised God for being "a refuge from the storm"—a wall that protected the poor and needy from the wrath of enemies and oppressors.

Few of us live near a desert, so few of us know the relief

that comes with safely riding out a sandstorm. But each of us has experienced the Lord's protection when the winds of adversity have howled around us.

Trust God that He can and will be there for you again when you need Him most.

## FOR FURTHER THOUGHT

Have you ever been "caught in the storm," unprepared for tragedy and blinded by the sands of grief and bitterness? If so, how did you escape?

How might a Christian prepare for heartbreak, even the kind that comes suddenly? How effective is this preparation?

## PRAYER

*Lord, give me a solid plan for running to You when life kicks up dust. Prepare me for the worst so that I can live for the best.*

## — 40 —

# BASIC LIFE LESSONS

*"But ask the animals, and they will teach you,*
*or the birds in the sky, and they will tell you*
*. . .or let the fish in the sea inform you."*
JOB 12:7–8 NIV

This verse is not saying that we should be like Dr. Doolittle and talk with animals. Job's counselors had been lecturing him on the basics of cause and effect, insisting that suffering often implies punishment for sin. "Who does not know all these things?" Job asked (Job 12:3 NIV). Then he pointed them to *other* basics: that sometimes, the innocent suffer while the cruel triumph. For examples, look no further than the animal kingdom.

Men and women are not brute beasts caught up in a mere survival of the fittest—the grace of God intervenes constantly in our lives. But as living beings, we too are subject to the influences of a sin-spoiled world. . .and suffer as a result. Even innocent fawns are maimed in accidents. Even trees die of disease.

We should live righteous lives, but there's no guarantee that doing so will spare us from being touched by the pain and suffering of this world.

## FOR FURTHER THOUGHT

Given all the suffering in this life, it hardly seems fair. How does the existence of an eternal home with God balance the scales?

God calls us to leave matters of fairness and justice to Him. How do things like revenge and bitterness only make things worse, even when we feel we're making things better?

What reassurance is there in knowing that our suffering isn't always connected to our sin?

## PRAYER

*Righteous God, I don't have an answer for life's tragedies. . . other than that You do. And that's all the answer I need.*

## — 41 —

# THAT YOU CARE FOR ME

*Lord, what are human beings that you care for them, mere mortals that you think of them?*
Psalm 144:3 NIV

The biblical Sea of Galilee is known by locals as the Sea of Genneseret or Lake Kinneret. It's located in the Galilee region in northern Israel, fed by underground streams and the famous Jordan River, which cuts north to south through the sea.

In ages past, God knew civilization would follow the trail of water—so He placed Genneseret strategically to provide for people. Christ performed miracles and preached to thousands along its shore. And as you hike your trail of life, know that the God who knew you before you were even conceived planned similar places for you to stop and partake of His living water.

Choose the path prepared by the Creator long before

mankind walked on earth. Along its way He has placed people to encourage, assist, and teach you His ways. God thought of you, cared for you, and provided for your every need.

## FOR FURTHER THOUGHT

Are there any people, places, or events in your life that serve as metaphorical "Seas of Galilee"—providing rest and encouragement when you need it most?

How might knowing that the placement of a body of water was intentional comfort you whenever you face a frustrating and confusing problem?

## PRAYER

*Lord Jesus, You came down and walked upon the landscape You'd so meticulously crafted. . .all for our redemption. Thank You for Your care.*

# — 42 —

# OBEDIENCE BRINGS SUCCESS

*Ants are creatures of little strength,*
*yet they store up their food in the summer.*
PROVERBS 30:25 NIV

Ants have something going for them that we don't: they lack an inclination toward selfishness! Their teamwork can be seen all over the outdoors.

In some climates, ants make their nests and tunnels entirely underground. But in areas where clay soils drain poorly, they build hills of leaf stems, evergreen tree needles, and sand. They carry each curious item from wherever they find it on their travels.

The hill makes a nest and tunnel system that rises above rain puddles and deflects any drops that fall on its domed top. As weather permits, these industrious creatures enlarge and maintain their hill. Long-established hills are often overspread by moss or grasses until only their shape gives them away.

Wherever they live, ants cooperate to gather their food when it's available. They seem to function as if the entire colony were controlled by one mind.

What a picture for us as believers, to work together as if we are controlled by one mind—the mind of Jesus Christ.

## FOR FURTHER THOUGHT

Unlike the ants, human have to strive to cooperate—it doesn't come naturally to us. Why is it so difficult for us to get along?

How might a good church resemble a strong anthill?

What other examples of determined teamwork can you find in nature?

## PRAYER

*God, thank You for giving us the ant to observe and learn from. Give me patience, determination, and love to work with others in advancing Your goals.*

## — 43 —

# JESUS CALMS THE STORM

*Jesus was in the stern, sleeping on a cushion. The disciples woke him and said to him, "Teacher, don't you care if we drown?" He got up, rebuked the wind and said to the waves, "Quiet! Be still!" Then the wind died down and it was completely calm.*

MARK 4:38–39 NIV

Viewing a large body of water can be a sublime experience. Some resemble huge bowls of gelatin, their placid surface unmarred by a single ripple. Others rage like angry beasts bent on destruction. For the latter, it takes a well-built ship with securely sealed hatches and portals to stay above the surface.

One time, the apostles—many of them experienced sailors—were terrified in a storm at sea. . .all while Jesus slept. Isn't that a poignant description of our lives? As waves of despair beat down, we wonder if Jesus is sleeping. We want Him to wake up and calm our storms immediately; otherwise, we fear we'll go down with the ship.

But faith makes our boat watertight. As long as we ensure our trust is in the Master of the waves, we are protected from the storm.

## FOR FURTHER THOUGHT

Do you think Jesus slept because He was tired, because He wanted to teach His disciples something, or both?

What do you think would have happened if the disciples hadn't awakened Jesus?

Do you ever feel like God is letting your life get out of hand? Have you ever tried to "wake Him up" or, even worse, taken matters into your own hands? If so, how did that turn out?

## PRAYER

*Lord Jesus, just as the disciples were safe as long as You were in the boat, I know I'm safe as long as You're in my life.*

## — 44 —

# INTELLIGENT DESIGNER

*"Is it your wisdom that makes the hawk soar*
*and spread its wings toward the south?*
*Is it at your command that the eagle rises*
*to the heights to make its nest?"*
JOB 39:26–27 NLT

Sometimes, we need to be reminded who's in charge. With all our scientific advances, our ability to genetically engineer and clone living beings, people start thinking we're pretty hot. The end of such conceit is to think that we don't need God—that we are, in fact, nearly gods ourselves.

Scientists may be able to clone a hawk or an eagle, but all they're really doing is tinkering with an elaborate, astonishingly complex system already in place—a living being created by a designer whose "understanding is infinite" (Psalm 147:5 SKJV).

Only the infinitely intelligent Creator could design the

DNA of the hawk so that it would instinctively soar on high thermals and engineer eagles' genes so that thousands of generations of these magnificent birds would build their nests in lofty treetops and mountain crags.

Without a designer, there would be no design!

## FOR FURTHER THOUGHT

Humans can experiment with, alter, or even engineer biological life, but there's one thing they can't create or change: the soul. Why?

How does mankind's increasing capability to mimic the designs found in nature strengthen the case for a Creator?

How can Christians ensure they never fall victim to pride while utilizing the laws of nature in creative new ways?

## PRAYER

*Lord, human beings are just children playing in the sandbox of Your creation. Help me never to forget how reliant I am on You for everything.*

## — 45 —

# A TALE OF TWO WATERFALLS

*Then those who gladly received [Peter's] word were baptized, and the same day about three thousand souls were added to them.*

Acts 2:41 SKJV

Straddling the border of the United States and Canada, Niagara Falls is North America's most famous cataract. Millions have visited the thundering attraction, some 3,600 feet wide and 160 feet high.

Few but locals, however, know of the Dundee Falls in northeast Ohio. In a peaceful wood, a small stream trickles over a rock ledge to a pool some fifteen feet below. It's tame and quiet, nothing like the mighty Niagara.

So which is better? That's a subjective question. Both were created by God, and each has undoubtedly pointed people to Him. The two waterfalls are just *different*—much the way people are.

In the early church, the mighty, thundering Peter once pointed three thousand souls to Jesus. But those nameless individuals—the "tame and quiet" bunch—formed the backbone of the church we're part of today.

If you're not a Peter, don't think you're unimportant. Not every waterfall is a Niagara. But every one of us has a special, God-given job to do.

## FOR FURTHER THOUGHT

What's your unique talent or area of interest? Have you worked on honing this particular skill or passion?

How might you utilize that ability or enthusiasm in working for God?

## PRAYER

*God, maybe You want me to be a thundering Niagara, declaring Your power—or perhaps a gentle stream, radiating Your love. Either way, I'm willing to be used.*

## — 46 —

# EARTHLY PARADISE. . . MADE PERFECT

*He made known to us the mystery of his will according to his good pleasure. . .to be put into effect when the times reach their fulfillment—to bring unity to all things in heaven and on earth under Christ.*

EPHESIANS 1:9–10 NIV

It's probably safe to say that most Christians who've enjoyed the natural beauty of God's created world have also found their thoughts directed toward heaven and eternal perfection.

We Christians can enjoy the wonders of the created world—but we also know the biblical truth that what was once perfect was thrown into chaos when sin entered the garden of Eden. There are wonderful promises, though, in God's written Word. One day, all things will be restored to their original state of perfection.

Imagine for a moment your very favorite places on earth—places in which you spend time enjoying the natural beauty God has created for you. Then imagine those places as not only pleasant but absolutely perfect. . .just like you will one day be in Jesus Christ.

## FOR FURTHER THOUGHT

Why do you think God has wired humans to feel awe at natural landscapes and phenomena? Could this instinct be pointing us to something deeper?

When you think of heaven, what comes to mind? How does it feel knowing that even your wildest imaginations can't hold a candle to heaven's actual beauty?

## PRAYER

*Father, in light of the breathtaking mysteries of the natural world, I can only marvel and guess at the supernatural blessings You've prepared. Thank You.*

## — 47 —

# OUTDOOR STEWARDSHIP

*"The earth is the Lord's,*
*and everything in it."*
1 Corinthians 10:26 niv

Most people, when using someone else's stuff—whether it's a camera, a car, or camping equipment—treat those things with special care, probably far greater care than we show toward our own.

But what about the outdoors itself? The Bible clearly teaches that the earth we enjoy, including the outdoors, belongs to God—and that He's given all of it to us to treat with an attitude of respect and stewardship. That means we should feel free to *use* all God has given us to enjoy. . .but never to *misuse* it.

We are all free to enjoy God's creation—whether it's through fishing, hunting, hiking, camping, or mountain biking. But let's never forget that the outdoors we enjoy belongs to God Himself. . .and that we should treat it with the respect due to His "stuff."

## FOR FURTHER THOUGHT

How might many Christians' treatment of the environment reveal their beliefs about God's relationship with His creation?

Do you ever litter, or do you go out of your way to properly dispose of waste? Why?

## PRAYER

*Lord, thank You for entrusting us with this wild, breathtaking planet we call home. Help me do my part to preserve the beauty You've given.*

## — 48 —

# DOWN BY THE RIVERSIDE

*They are like trees planted along the riverbank,*
*bearing fruit each season. Their leaves never*
*wither, and they prosper in all they do.*
PSALM 1:3 NLT

Viewing the valley below, you can see clearly where the river runs—its path is lined with trees. Farmlands and orchards surround this winding, narrow path. Farther up the valley, however, the trees and lush greenery fade, giving way to scattered vegetation and dry, brown grass. The effect of the water is clear: Proximity to it allows life to flourish. Distance makes it harder.

Unlike those trees, we can choose where we're planted—either close to God or far away. The psalm writer tells us that choosing to walk in the path of the righteous makes us like a tree planted near the river. There, we find life-giving water that feeds our soul and causes us to grow tall and full in the Lord. We become green trees bearing good fruit.

Where do you want to be planted? Which way will you choose to walk today?

## FOR FURTHER THOUGHT

How far or close would you consider yourself to be in relation to the river of God's righteousness?

What are some ways you can inch closer to His life-giving waters today?

## PRAYER

*Thank You, Lord, for giving us a river from which we can draw our strength. May my roots always dig deeper into Your banks, searching for more nutrients.*

# — 49 —

# THE CENTER OF IT ALL

*From heaven the* Lord *looks down and sees all mankind.*
Psalm 33:13 niv

From the middle of an ocean, we get an unusual perspective. Beyond sight of land, the horizon is a straight line between sea and sky—turn a complete circle, and the line goes with you. If the sea is calm, the horizon often seems higher, giving us the effect of being at the bottom of a shallow saucer, or perhaps at the focal point of a lens.

It can be a lonely experience, or it can make us feel like the world revolves around us, like we are the center of it all. Strangely, both feelings are true.

In a world of eight billion people, it is possible to be entirely alone, both physically and emotionally. Yet each one of us is the focus of God's attention. In His infinite power and love, He sees nothing more important in the universe than individual human beings.

That's a sobering thought when we're contemplating a tough moral choice. But it's an incredibly comforting thought when we feel far from shore.

## FOR FURTHER THOUGHT

How does being physically alone for a while often bring a Christian closer to God?

Why does God care so much about humanity, given the vast size of the planet and the universe it inhabits?

When you feel alone, what brings your mind back to God's care?

## PRAYER

*Omnipresent Lord, this world is just too big sometimes. . . I'm surrounded by emptiness, and nobody seems to care. Thank You for being my committed traveling companion.*

## — 50 —

# ESCAPING TO A MOUNTAIN

*In the* L*ORD* *I take refuge. How then can you say to me: "Flee like a bird to your mountain"?*

PSALM 11:1 NIV

Birds often build their nests in high trees or in the clefts of mountainsides. When attacked, they'll flee to their refuge.

When some of David's worried advisors warned him to retreat to some wilderness stronghold to escape his enemies' conspiracy, David insisted that he would take refuge in the Lord. In Psalm 18:2 (NIV), David said, "The LORD is my rock, my fortress, and my deliverer; my God is my rock, in whom I take refuge." David would flee like a bird to his mountain—but this rock fortress was spiritual. He would stay right where he was, trusting God to protect him.

When we know we're doing God's will—when we're right where we should be—we can trust God to protect us. We're not easily scared off. We may waver and be tempted to retreat to some "safer" place, but as long as God is with us, our best course of action is to stand our ground.

## FOR FURTHER THOUGHT

Have you ever found refuge from a storm inside a cave or rock cleft? In what ways is God's protection even better?

How do you reach your "spiritual safe place" with God?

## PRAYER

*Lord, I don't want to put my trust in earthly hideouts. Rocks can crumble and houses can fall, but only Your promises can weather all storms.*

## — 51 —

# A SMALL TASTE OF PARADISE

*Jesus answered him, "Truly I tell you, today you will be with me in paradise."*
LUKE 23:43 NIV

We who enjoy the great, God-given outdoors sometimes refer to our favorite locations as "heaven on earth."

But think for a minute about the most beautiful natural place you've ever visited, and remember that it's only a foreshadowing of the beauty you'll enjoy with your Savior in heaven.

When Jesus told the penitent criminal that he would soon see paradise, He hinted at the profound, eternal joy that awaits those who trust and follow the Lord. Think about it: if God in the flesh—the Creator of all the natural beauty we enjoy—calls a place "paradise," its beauty must outshine anything our mortal minds could fathom!

Right now, we're experiencing only a small taste of "paradise."

## FOR FURTHER THOUGHT

How often do you dwell on your future eternal home? Would it help to envision paradise, despite knowing all your imaginations will fall short?

Why do you think God has hidden the secrets of paradise from us while we're on this earth? What do you think would happen to someone who saw even a glimpse of them in this life?

## PRAYER

*Father, Your amazing creation gives me the slightest hint of what heaven will be like. Help me to keep the fire of awe alive in my heart.*

## — 52 —

# THE BEGINNING OF CREATION

*"And write to the angel of the church of the Laodiceans: 'The Amen, the faithful and true witness, the beginning of the creation of God, says these things.'"*

REVELATION 3:14 SKJV

Stargazing has always been a fascinating pastime for us earthlings. We stand in awe looking at the Milky Way. We contemplate the Big and Little Dippers, Orion's Belt, and many other constellations. We thrill over eclipses and shooting stars.

Since the Hubble telescope became operational in the early 1990s, we've marveled at breathtaking photographs from deep space. It's possible to have a spiritual experience viewing God's handiwork in these images.

As wonderful as the Hubble telescope is, however, none of its combined technology and equipment can match the optics God created in the human eye. But even the incredible eye—as it exists now—can't absorb God's magnificence or comprehend "the beginning of the creation of God," our Lord Jesus Christ.

## FOR FURTHER THOUGHT

It's been said the most beautiful thing in the universe is our ability to observe it. What use would all the stars in the universe have if nobody were around to see them?

At the end of time, God will give us minds and eyes that will be able to observe something even greater than the universe: Himself. How eager are you to obtain this amazing understanding?

## PRAYER

*Lord, if this fallen world is enough to strike awe and reverent fear into my soul, I can only imagine the beauties that await in Your perfect eternity.*

## — 53 —

# GOD OF THE STORM

*The voice of the* Lord *twists the oaks and strips the forests bare. And in his temple all cry, "Glory!"*

Psalm 29:9 niv

If you've ever hiked through the woods during a powerful thunderstorm, you know the mixture of fear and awe that such a storm can evoke. The thunder rattles our bones, and we keep a watchful eye on the writhing oaks above us, hoping they can withstand the onslaught of wind.

Such awe is no doubt a mere glimpse of the wonder that the heavenly beings must experience every moment in the presence of the God who made the storms. This is the God who simply spoke the world into existence (Genesis 1), and He sustains it by His powerful Word (Hebrews 1:3). Yet even in His greatness, He continues to care for His people, granting them strength and peace (Psalm 29:11).

The next time you're caught outside in a storm, take a moment to praise the Creator of the storm—and rest in His great care for His people.

## FOR FURTHER THOUGHT

Storms are beautiful. . .until we're caught in them. How does remembering the Maker and Master of the storm bring calm?

How is the glory of God similar to a raging storm? How is it different? What should be our reaction when we're presented with a taste of His splendor?

## PRAYER

*Father, I'm unable to fathom the strange beauties and terrors that surround Your majesty. But I know You love me, so I take comfort in Your greatness.*

## — 54 —

# STRANGE THINGS IN THE SEA

*O* Lord, *how manifold are your works! In wisdom have you made them all. . . . Here is the sea, great and wide, which teems with creatures innumerable, living things both small and great.*

Psalm 104:24–25 ESV

Scientists are still finding astonishing things in the sea—"living things both small and great"—from two-hundred-foot-long jellyfish to stubby-limbed octopi to alien creatures making their homes near sulfuric heat vents in the total darkness of the ocean's floor. Scientists have even discovered shrimp residing in the Mariana Trench—nearly seven miles down!

In the twenty-first century, dozens of new ocean species are still being discovered every year. Some of them are extremely odd, yet all of them are perfectly suited to the harsh and improbable environment they call home. The very existence of these creatures proclaims the handiwork of an intelligent Creator.

God not only designed the exotic life forms that inhabit the depths of the sea—He designed human life as well. And like these other amazing life forms, we exist to manifest the wisdom and glory of God.

## FOR FURTHER THOUGHT

These creatures may not be conscious of their Creator—but we certainly are. How is this knowledge changing the way you live?

How has God equipped you to adapt, like the meticulously designed creatures in the sea, to whatever life throws your way?

## PRAYER

*Lord, thank You for populating this earth with such a wide variety of creations. May my life be yet another proof of Your creativity and power.*

## — 55 —

# ANCIENT AGRICULTURAL PARABLES

*For as the soil makes the sprout come up and a garden causes seeds to grow, so the Sovereign Lord will make righteousness and praise spring up before all nations.*

Isaiah 61:11 niv

Salvation and our righteousness are gifts from God. They are His work in our lives. God brings them about; we simply open our hearts to receive them. As Isaiah 45:8 (niv) says beautifully, "You heavens above, rain down my righteousness. . . . Let the earth open wide, let salvation spring up, let righteousness flourish with it."

The ancient Israelites were intimately linked to the land and dependent upon the annual rains. And just as they knew it was God who sent rain and provided soil in which seeds grew, they also understood that it was God who showered down His righteousness, causing crops of salvation and praise to spring up in their lives.

Jesus taught similar ideas in the parable of the sower, urging us to receive His Word "with a noble and good heart" (Luke 8:15 NIV). That's the way to really enjoy salvation!

## FOR FURTHER THOUGHT

Have you ever experienced a time of spiritual drought? If so, how did this experience increase your appreciation of the rains when they finally came?

Are you seeking out God's water, asking Him daily to send it down, or are you content to let time and chance decide if you grow?

## PRAYER

*Father, keep sending down Your blessings. And if the river starts to dry up, grow my roots so that they find You in deeper places.*

## — 56 —

# OUTDOOR EQUIPMENT

*So God created man in His own image,*
*in the image of God He created him;*
*male and female He created them.*
GENESIS 1:27 SKJV

Technology keeps improving our outdoor equipment, from the mountain bikes and four-wheelers we ride to the GPS systems that tell us how to get back home.

But our most amazing equipment has always been right with us: the human body, handcrafted by God. Think of everything the body does on a simple hike: The legs propel the body forward, adjusting effortlessly to changes in terrain. Arms and hands provide balance and aid progress on particularly challenging trails. Eyes and ears take in the stimuli of the woods—the colors of the leaves, the sounds of the birds—and the brain analyzes that data without slowing the ongoing physical processes in the slightest.

Meanwhile, our conscious thoughts run from family to work to church to that funny movie we just saw. . .and maybe, if we're lucky, to that gallon of milk we were asked to pick up on the way home.

There will never be a machine to compare with the human body!

## FOR FURTHER THOUGHT

Given that God wants us to care for nature, how much more does He expect us to care for His most amazing creation of all: our bodies?

What do you think "the image of God" refers to: awareness, free will, rationality, or a mixture of all three? Why?

## PRAYER

*Lord, thank You for equipping me with the tools I need to observe Your creation—and the mind to know it all came from You.*

## — 57 —

# JOINING CREATION IN PRAISING GOD

*"You will go out in joy and be led forth in peace;*
*the mountains and hills will burst into song before you,*
*and all the trees of the field will clap their hands."*

ISAIAH 55:12 NIV

Think about this: the scenery and the sounds you enjoy in the outdoors are a means by which God allows the whole earth to speak praises to His name.

God created the world around us to serve as our temporal home, but He also created it to glorify Himself. It truly serves as a beacon of praise to the entire universe. God made all of creation itself not just for us to enjoy it but for us to joyfully praise Him.

The next time you're out in the woods, on a mountaintop, or near a river, stop to soak in the view and listen to the beautiful sounds of nature. Remember that God created and sustains all those things—then join creation in praising His wonderful name!

## FOR FURTHER THOUGHT

Fellowship with other Christians is important, but communing with God in nature can be just as rewarding. Do you regularly try to do both?

Do you take the natural sights and sounds all around you for granted, or are you intentional in your experience of them, working to glean the spiritual from what some see as the mundane?

## PRAYER

*Lord, the heavens and earth praise Your name. Open my ears to their cry, and then open my mouth so that I can join them in worship.*

## — 58 —

# RAVAGED, MAJESTIC FORESTS

*Even the junipers and the cedars of Lebanon gloat over you and say, "Now that you have been laid low, no one comes to cut us down."*

Isaiah 14:8 NIV

The towering cedar tree with its spreading branches is so majestic that Lebanon has adopted it as her symbol, emblazing the tree upon her flag. This Middle Eastern country has been famous for its cedars for millennia—its mountains were once thickly cloaked with forests.

No more. Centuries of logging have left only scattered cedar groves, and callous conquerors have ravaged Lebanon's forests to build siege towers, palaces, and fleets of warships. The Assyrians boasted, "I have cut down its tallest cedars" (Isaiah 37:24 NIV). No wonder that after the Assyrians fell, the trees were said to rejoice.

Today, we need wood to build our homes and furniture,

but more and more Christians are realizing the need to conserve natural resources and heritage areas for future generations. We don't have to be tree huggers, but God *does* call us to consider others' needs—to be good stewards of the world He's put in our care.

## FOR FURTHER THOUGHT

How do you think God feels when humans treat the beauties of His creation like they're worthless? How would you feel if someone marred your most prized creation?

What precautions can you realistically take to help preserve God's creation? What measures are you taking right now?

## PRAYER

*God, I don't worship Your creation. . .but I do believe appreciating Your creation is one way of worshipping You. May I treat it with reverence and responsibility.*

## 59

# A STEADY LIGHT

*He leads the humble in what is right,*
*and teaches the humble his way.*
PSALM 25:9 ESV

Can you find the Big Dipper in the night sky? The two stars at the leading edge of the ladle are known as "pointer stars." If you draw an imaginary line from the bottom pointer through the top and keep going, the next star you'll meet is Polaris, the Pole Star.

Throughout history, the Pole Star has given northern travelers their bearings. Columbus used it as he voyaged west. Marco Polo watched it as he ventured east.

We may feel a kinship with previous generations as we gaze upon a steady light that they, too, saw in their night sky. But our souls have a deeper kinship with the Creator of Polaris and all the other stars. The motion of the universe may eventually remove Polaris from true north—but God will always be here, showing us the perfect direction in which to travel.

## FOR FURTHER THOUGHT

What reasons do you think God had for giving the stars a practical function?

How might looking at the stars give us an understanding—however weak—of God's eternal nature?

## PRAYER

*Father, thank You for being more reliable than Polaris—more steadfast than the most ancient constellation. I trust in You, who made the stars.*

## — 60 —

# SEEING THE INVISIBLE

*For since the creation of the world God's invisible qualities—his eternal power and divine nature—have been clearly seen, being understood from what has been made.*

ROMANS 1:20 NIV

Ansel Adams was a photographer best known for his black-and-white images of natural scenery in the American West, particularly California's Yosemite National Park. You don't have to look long at a collection of Adams' art to know that he loved Yosemite's natural beauty.

Just as we can learn a lot about artists or photographers—about what is really important to them—by looking at their work, we can learn a lot about God by studying the awesomeness of the world He created.

Next time you have a chance to see a towering mountain range, a pristine tract of forest, a meandering river, or any other example of nature's beauty, consider them not only as valuable and beautiful natural resources but as reflections of the magnificence, beauty, and goodness of the God who, with just His spoken word, made them to reflect Himself.

## FOR FURTHER THOUGHT

Whether Ansel Adams intended it or not, his works are valuable tools for proclaiming God's glory. How are you using your talents to do the same?

Why do you think so many people fail to see God in creation?

## PRAYER

*Lord, when I see the wonders of the natural world, I see the wonders of Your supernatural power. Thank You for these captivating glimpses.*

# — 61 —

# SOGGY-SANDALED SOVEREIGN

*And they came to Him and awoke Him, saying, "Master, Master, we are perishing!" Then He arose and rebuked the wind and the raging of the water. And they ceased, and there was a calm.*

LUKE 8:24 SKJV

Who can control the waves? Most of us wouldn't try. But legend has it that Canute, an English king, had his throne placed by the shore. He sat there and commanded the waves not to wet his feet. Of course, he got soaked.

Historians debate whether he was serious in his intent or whether he was trying to teach his courtiers a lesson in humility. Either way, he hung his gold crown shortly afterward on a crucifix and left it there to show the King of kings was more powerful than any ordinary king.

It sounds like Canute was not as foolish as the legend makes him seem. He knew that while no earthly power—then or now—could control the waves, there once was a Man who did just that.

## FOR FURTHER THOUGHT

Have you ever tried to control something in your life, only to concede defeat by admitting your helplessness? What do you learn from such a circumstance?

How might such moments of weakness help us remember God's strength?

## PRAYER

*Lord, some things are out of my control. . .and that's okay. Just as I trust You to control the waves, I trust You to control my life.*

## — 62 —

# GRANDEUR OF GOD'S CREATION

*Who has measured the waters in the hollow of his hand,*
*or with the breadth of his hand marked off the heavens?*
*Who has held the dust of the earth in a basket, or weighed*
*the mountains on the scales and the hills in a balance?*

Isaiah 40:12 NIV

Focused on the pressing responsibilities of life, it's easy to forget the infinite greatness of God. That's why He tells us to meditate on what He's said. Sometimes, it's easier to do that outdoors.

A change of scenery can broaden our perspective on life, unveiling the unmistakable evidence of God's power and wisdom. At the seashore, the ocean's vast, curving horizon displays the enormity of God's creation. The plains offer a similar though unique testimony, humbling us with the Lord's greatness. And looking down from a mountaintop has caused many believers to breathe out the classic lyrics,

"How great Thou art!"

Even Jesus took time to retreat for rest to the mountains—so why shouldn't we?

The Creator of all things wants us to recognize His greatness and praise Him for it. Our peace and confidence grow in proportion to our understanding of God's power.

## FOR FURTHER THOUGHT

Beauty is often subjective, meaning one person may admire a landscape while another overlooks it. What unique beauties captivate your eyes and point you toward God?

How can a Christian avoid "missing the forest for the trees"—overlooking God's beautiful design and focusing instead on the tiny, seemingly unappealing details found within?

What are some things in life that are meant to be simply enjoyed and not controlled?

## PRAYER

*Lord, I never want to miss the beauty of Your masterpieces by obsessing over the details. Teach me how to appreciate Your art and revel in Your glory.*

## — 63 —

# THE REALITY OF HEAVEN

*However, as it is written: "What no eye has seen, what no ear has heard, and what no human mind has conceived"—the things God has prepared for those who love him.*

1 Corinthians 2:9 NIV

Vacations take planning. Many of us pore over brochures or Internet sites, trying to decide exactly where we want to go. Finally, we narrow our choice down to that one spot that creates the most excitement—say, for example, the Grand Canyon.

When the big day arrives, we take to the road with great anticipation. At first, the miles pass quickly. . .but before long, the trip seems to slow. All this "fun" actually becomes tiring.

We verify our route a hundred times. The road goes up and down, curving and twisting amid myriads of pesky hills and rivers. We stop to eat and rest then try to make up for lost time. But deep down, we know we're getting closer with every mile. . .and so the excitement starts to return.

At last, we arrive and impatiently make our way to the rim, where the view immediately takes our breath away. It's more than the pictures revealed, more than we ever imagined.

Multiply that excitement by a zillion times for a preview of heaven.

## FOR FURTHER THOUGHT

Have you ever wished the road to heaven were shorter? Why do you think God allows us to wander with blistered feet for so long before reaching home?

In what way does the brief but rewarding vacation in today's illustration fundamentally differ from the joy of heaven?

## PRAYER

*Lord, thank You for promising an eternal paradise at the end of this long, winding road. Help me stay on this path until the end.*

## — 64 —

# WHERE WATER NEVER CEASES

*"Does the snow of Lebanon leave the crags of Sirion? Do the mountain waters run dry, the cold flowing streams? But my people have forgotten me."*

JEREMIAH 18:14–15 ESV

We often focus on the beauty of the outdoors, and justifiably so—God's creation is clearly something to marvel over. But His creation is also practical.

Sirion, also known as Mount Hermon, can experience snow on its peak during summer. As the snow melts, it runs down the mountain, providing an abundance of water for drinking or planting crops. In Bible times, this was an ideal environment—a place where the waters didn't run dry. No sane person would want to leave such a place.

So why do we do that with God? Though He provides for our every need, we often stray from Him. We leave His mountain in search of even more—only to find out that other places are in decay, void of living water.

Today, listen for God's call to remain on His mountain, basking in His excellent provision.

## FOR FURTHER THOUGHT

Think of a place that was so glorious that you wanted to stay there forever. Do you spend as much time with God as you would in that place if you never had to leave?

What do you think is the main reason people leave God? How can you make sure this never happens to you?

## PRAYER

*Father, You've made Your creation both beautiful and practical—just like our relationship to You. Help me never to walk away from the goodness You provide.*

# — 65 —

## TAKE THE PLUNGE

*Then the angel showed me the river of the water of life, as clear as crystal.*
REVELATION 22:1 NIV

A hot summer day at a park in the mountains wouldn't be complete without a dip in the river.

Cool, clear water runs in this river, and the swimming hole is deep enough for diving. You've just returned from a long, dusty hike, so the water looks more inviting than a five-star buffet. You quickly remove your gear, change into your swimming suit. . .and jump. Breaking the surface, your whole body feels chilled, refreshed, and strangely cleansed. As you push off the rocky bottom to come back up for air, you feel marvelously alive.

Diving into a relationship with God can be like that. Covered with the dust, sweat, and grime of a day in the world, you can dive deeply into time with your Creator and

Savior. Bring your cares, problems, and concerns to Jesus in quiet prayer. Lay them at His feet and immerse yourself in His love.

## FOR FURTHER THOUGHT

Which spiritual activity makes you feel closest to God? Throughout the day, how often do you think of this activity?

Do you treat time with God like it's a chore rather than a treat? If so, how might you change that attitude?

## PRAYER

*Lord, thank You for the spiritually refreshing peace You offer at the end of a long day. May I never tire of this wonderful feeling.*

# — 66 —

# SHARK CAGE

*"Be strong and of good courage. Do not be afraid or be dismayed, for the* Lord *your God is with you wherever you go."*

Joshua 1:9 skjv

If you ever have the privilege of visiting Australia's Great Barrier Reef, you'll see that it's full of examples of God's creation.

Shark encounters are common in the reef, usually with gray nurse sharks that pose no threat to swimmers. Since they're well fed from the abundance of fish in the area, they pay little attention to humans. For more adventure, though, you can go farther out into the ocean, where the great white sharks concentrate. But you'll want to be in a shark cage.

From the safety of the cage, you can see these magnificent creatures up close—and realize just how fearsome they are. Your safety depends on those metal bars surrounding you—without them, you'd be in trouble.

We live in a world full of trouble, and there are plenty of "sharks" just waiting to attack and eat us alive. In God's presence, though, we can know that we'll always be protected from harm.

## FOR FURTHER THOUGHT

What kind of "sharks" threaten your physical, emotional, and spiritual well-being?

What types of protective "bars" does God offer to you? How are you using them?

## PRAYER

*Lord, I thank You for watching over me and protecting me from the predators of this world.*

# — 67 —

# TRASH ON THE WATER

*Religion that God our Father accepts as pure and faultless is this: to look after orphans and widows in their distress and to keep oneself from being polluted by the world.*

JAMES 1:27 NIV

The television news reporter stood by a lake as she discussed the problem of pollution. Countless people had visited the lake to fish, swim, and enjoy its beauty. . .leaving trash behind them in the water and on the shore.

As the people's carelessness compounded, the situation reached a breaking point. Before long, the whole area felt dirty. Ugliness stained the once pleasant getaway. The entire lake was tainted.

A sad story? Absolutely. And it's one that can happen to even the best of us. Just as any amount of garbage can contaminate a large recreational area, a little bit of sin can destroy our whole lives.

## FOR FURTHER THOUGHT

Do you feel annoyed when people litter, especially in places that are known for their natural beauty? How do you think God feels when we pollute our souls with sin?

How does a polluted soul impact not only us and God but the people who see us?

## PRAYER

*Lord, I want to be a pure reflection of Your glory. Purge me of the stains and grunge that threaten to mar my testimony.*

## — 68 —

# THIRSTY FOR GOD

*As the deer pants for the water brooks,*
*so my soul pants for You, O God. My soul*
*thirsts for God, for the living God.*
PSALM 42:1–2 SKJV

Three kinds of deer—the red deer, the spotted fallow deer, and the roe deer—were once a common sight in Israel's forests and wilderness. As the sun beat down all day, deer became very thirsty. Flowing brooks were few and far between, but the deer knew exactly where they were.

When David saw these deer stop grazing, compelled to seek out a brook to slake their thirst, he saw echoes of his own thirst for God. For David, taking time to "tank up" on God was not simply a religious duty—it was a pressing need. He could never be too busy for God.

Thousands of years have passed, and our world is as dry and thirsty as ever. While many religions promise spiritual refreshment, there is still only one true source of flowing, life-giving water—our living God.

## FOR FURTHER THOUGHT

Have you ever gone without water for a lengthy period of time? If so, how might this experience help you better understand the desperation implicit in today's verse?

Just as God placed the instinct of thirst inside all living things, He has placed a thirst for Him inside of us. Are you following or suppressing this instinct?

## PRAYER

*Lord, for all its promises of satisfaction, this world is nothing but a dried riverbed. Lead me to Your living waters, where I can find true, eternal peace.*

## — 69 —

# TUMBLEWEEDS

*Make them like tumbleweed, my God, like chaff before the wind. As fire consumes the forest or a flame sets the mountains ablaze, so pursue them with your tempest and terrify them with your storm. Cover their faces with shame,* LORD, *so that they will seek your name.*

PSALM 83:13–16 NIV

On the North Texas plains, tumbleweeds roll across the flat ground, propelled by the strong, dry wind. Most bushes and trees are firmly rooted below the surface—but tumbleweeds, in a stiff wind, easily break off at the ground then roll along with the breeze.

The psalmist compares God's enemies to tumbleweeds. A tumbleweed bears no fruit. Its stalk quickly dries and becomes light and brittle. It's fit for nothing except the fire.

That's the kind of tree Jesus once described. "A good

tree cannot bear bad fruit, and a bad tree cannot bear good fruit. Every tree that does not bear good fruit is cut down and thrown into the fire. Thus, by their fruit you will recognize them" (Matthew 7:18–20 NIV).

What can you do today to avoid tumbleweed status?

## FOR FURTHER THOUGHT

Do you sometimes feel as if you're drifting like a tumbleweed—passionlessly going through the motions? What's one way you can rekindle your spiritual fire?

Tumbleweeds are stark reminders of the barren nature of a terrain. What signs of spiritual barrenness do you see in the culture today?

## PRAYER

*Lord God, I want to be a thriving tree, not a tumbleweed. Keep me forever supplied with Your life-giving nutrients and fasten my roots firmly within Your love.*

## — 70 —

# RESCUE THE PERISHING

*Deliver those who are drawn to death.*

Proverbs 24:11 SKJV

For one young boy, summer in the outdoors was paradise on earth. Otters in the river. Beavers building dams. Turtles sunning aside the lazy waters. Morning and evening, the concert of the birds. Every night, the distant grumble of the bullfrogs in the swamp.

But soon, the boy found trouble in Eden. Someone had speared eels and left them rotting on the rocks. Turtles had been shot and left along the path. Traps had been laid for beavers in the shallows of the riverbank.

One day, the boy found a groundhog caught in the metal teeth of a trap. He knew the animal would chew its leg off to get free—unless he found a way to free it himself. The animal was wary at first, but the boy was cautious. Finally, using a long stick, he managed to open the trap and let the groundhog go.

God wants us to "rescue the weak and the needy; deliver them" (Psalm 82:4 NIV). Far more important than animals are the weak among us—the orphans, the oppressed, the aged, and the unborn. Let's do what we can to minister to their needs.

## FOR FURTHER THOUGHT

Sometimes, it's easy for well-meaning Christians to lay more traps than they open. How does this happen? What are some ways to avoid it?

Often, it takes more than words to free someone from a trap of addiction, poverty, or regrets. How willing are you to get your hands dirty while helping others?

## PRAYER

*Father, in a perfect world, there would be no traps to open. But the world isn't perfect. Help me use the tools You've given me to bring liberation.*

## — 71 —

# THE GRASS THAT FOREVER GROWS

*Therefore, my dear brothers and sisters, stand firm. Let nothing move you. Always give yourselves fully to the work of the Lord, because you know that your labor in the Lord is not in vain.*

1 Corinthians 15:58 NIV

Think of how much time and attention mere grass demands. To maintain a good-looking lawn, we must work on it regularly, watering it to keep it nice and green. Watering it, however, makes it grow faster, which makes mowing the lawn and trimming weeds necessary. After that, the whole cycle starts again. And if we ever stop, the grass quickly becomes messy and the ugly weeds begin to dominate.

Such is our walk with the Lord. It takes regular work—frequent prayer and Bible reading for guidance—to keep our lives in line. A well-manicured relationship with Him is work. But this work is far more rewarding than keeping up a lawn!

## FOR FURTHER THOUGHT

Do you ever grow weary in your spiritual activities? During these times, how important is it to press through, even when the passion seems to be gone?

A well-manicured lawn benefits the people who live there and attracts positive attention. What benefits does a well-kept spiritual life have?

## PRAYER

*God, I want to maintain my walk with You. Help me trim the weeds of sin that threaten to hide the reflection of Your glory in my life.*

# — 72 —

## THE WONDERFUL WIND

*"The wind blows wherever it wants. Just as you can hear the wind but can't tell where it comes from or where it is going, so you can't explain how people are born of the Spirit."*

JOHN 3:8 NLT

It's said that in Hawaii, you can fully lean into the stiff winds at the Nuuanu Pali State Park. . .and not fall. Clearly, the wind is powerful stuff—and you don't need to go to Hawaii for evidence. Leaves rustle in a gentle breeze, window panes rattle in a howling storm, and buildings topple beneath frightening hurricanes.

Jesus said God's Holy Spirit is like the wind—invisible in itself yet showing powerful effects. When we were born again, the Spirit of God came into our lives. He comforts us in times of trial, helps us when we don't know how to pray, and gives us boldness when we have the opportunity to share the gospel.

And like the Hawaiian winds, the Spirit also holds us up when we're buffeted by temptation. Even better, whenever we sin, He *lifts* us up to the throne of the Father so that we can confess and receive forgiveness.

## FOR FURTHER THOUGHT

What are some other natural phenomena that are entirely invisible yet result in spectacular displays? How might these examples boost our faith in God?

When is the last time you threw all your weight onto God, trusting that He'd catch you?

Why is it sometimes hard to trust Jesus, even when we see the effects of His love and power all around us?

## PRAYER

*Father, I can't see Your love. I can't even see You. But I can see the wonders flowing from Your presence, and that's more than enough for me.*

# — 73 —

# JETS AND PEOPLE

*Then God said, "Let the land produce vegetation. . . . Let the water teem with living creatures. . . . Let the land produce living creatures. . . . Let us make mankind in our image."*

GENESIS 1:11, 20, 24, 26 NIV

A popular speaker on creation likes to discuss the complexity of living beings. Noting that a jumbo jet has more than six million parts, not one of which can fly on its own, he makes the point that it's only when those parts are correctly assembled that a jet functions as it should, lifting tons of passengers and baggage to heights above thirty-five thousand feet. It seems a miracle of invention that such a thing can happen at all.

The greater miracle, though, is the way God created *us*. We move, communicate, and think. And we adapt—if any of our "parts" are functioning incorrectly, the rest of our body can make adjustments automatically. How many machines can do that?

A jet plane is a wonderful invention, but nothing compared to a complex, living organism. Inventive minds conceive amazing machines from the resources God has provided—but *only* God can create life itself from nothing.

## FOR FURTHER THOUGHT

To extend the illustration, think of how much faith we put in the people who made the jet plane. How does nature give us even more reasons to trust God with our lives?

If God could design the human body, with all its infinite complexities, how much more capable do you think He is of working out the complexities in your life?

## PRAYER

*God, help me to see You in the details. May I never chalk up life's greatest wonders to chance, but instead use them as opportunities to glorify Your name.*

## — 74 —

# SONG OF THE STARS

*Praise him, sun and moon,*
*praise him, all you shining stars.*
PSALM 148:3 NIV

When is the last time you stood alone in the night, watching the stars?

God's handiwork can be millions of miles away—yet as close as a quiet moment in the backyard. The same stars that shone on King David, Christopher Columbus, and George Washington have shone since the creation of the heavens. . .and still point us to our powerful Lord today.

So many of us are caught up in the rat race, searching for peace but missing some of the quiet signposts to God's presence. The night sky holds a million secrets, and it waits for us to step away from this hectic world and reach for His hand.

If your life seems to be careening out of control, stop

the treadmill. Pull the power cord of your schedule for a while and listen to the song of the stars. Your Creator waits on you tonight.

## FOR FURTHER THOUGHT

What are some distractions that you can trim out of your life to better focus on God?

In what ways do the truths of God's Word resemble the stars in the heaven? In what ways do they differ?

## PRAYER

*Almighty God, nothing in my schedule could ever be more important than spending time with You. May I always take the time to dwell on Your grandeur.*

## — 75 —

# CAREFREE IN CHAOTIC TIMES

*"Behold the fowls of the air, for they do not sow; they neither reap nor gather into barns. Yet your heavenly Father feeds them. Aren't you much more valuable than they are?"*

MATTHEW 6:26 SKJV

Proverbs 6:8 (NIV) tells us to consider how the ant "stores its provisions in summer and gathers its food at harvest." Ants know winter is coming, and they work hard to meet those future needs.

Yet Jesus knew that we would tend to be preoccupied with the future, so He advised us to focus on one day at a time. He reminded us that even though birds don't gather and store, God provides for their needs.

Mind you, birds don't sit around doing nothing. Of course, birds work hard. They need to—some of them must eat 100 percent of their body weight each day. And parents feeding hungry chicks are constantly searching for food. But they don't fret about possibilities or food shortages or economic projections. They find resources, use them, and start afresh.

There's nothing wrong with having a long-term savings plan like the ants, but we should never let future possibilities derail our peace.

Work hard, trusting your finances and future to God.

## FOR FURTHER THOUGHT

How can a Christian strike a balance between short-term faith and long-term preparation? What does that look like in everyday life?

Have you ever worried about a potential disaster—a job loss, the death of a loved one, an illness? If so, how did that worry impact, or fail to impact, the future?

## PRAYER

*God, give me the right mix of faith and precaution. Help me make good plans, but help me to never put all my trust in these plans.*

# 76

# APPLES AND. . .APPLES

*"Every tree is known by its own fruit."*
LUKE 6:44 SKJV

The sluggish swamp contained a couple of small islands with spongy grass and a brush-choked peninsula that poked into the black backwater. At the end of the solid ground stood a tree that promised afternoon refreshment. Mark hadn't noticed it before. But now, he could see ripe red fruit even across the wide, brackish water. Apples! He couldn't wait to eat one.

Mark scrambled up a wooded hillside, climbed down into the wash, picked his way across wet tufts of thick reeds, and pushed through the undergrowth to where the tree stood.

But what a disappointment—they were crabapples, "sour enough to set a squirrel's teeth on edge and make a jay scream," as Henry David Thoreau succinctly described them.

We often work hard for shiny rewards that don't pay off. Good fruit is not a matter of what the eye sees but of the nature of the tree. If we are branches of Jesus, God's fruitful tree, we won't just look good—we'll bear fruit that feeds and refreshes many (see John 15:5–8).

## FOR FURTHER THOUGHT

Which concerns you the most: the thought of not measuring up to people's standards of what a Christian should be. . . or the thought of not measuring up to God's standards?

How can a rotten "Christian" be even more hurtful to the faith than a self-proclaimed unbeliever?

## PRAYER

*Lord God, examine my soul today to see if my fruit is real. . . or if it's just a pale imitation of the real thing. Make me genuine.*

## — 77 —

# THE LIGHT OF THE MOON

*God made two great lights—the greater light to govern the day and the lesser light to govern the night. He also made the stars.*

GENESIS 1:16 NIV

As second largest object in the sky, the moon has always fascinated humans. It's inspired poems, stories, songs, and movies—and has always been associated with romance. But despite all these references to its brilliance, the moon does not possess a light of its own. Its light is simply the reflection of the sun.

Even more interesting, the moon sometimes passes between the sun and the earth, partially eclipsing the great star and occasionally obscuring it altogether.

We Christians are a lot like the moon. We have no light of our own but are simply reflections of the light of the Son of God. We can either reflect the brilliance of His light or we can obscure His light—becoming dark ourselves in the process.

## FOR FURTHER THOUGHT

Even when eclipses happen, the sun still shines. Soon, its glory is revealed again—and every eye sees it. Similarly, how might God use proud people to bring glory to Himself?

When you accomplish something great or admirable, do you bask in the praise of others, or do you take the time to reflect the spotlight back to God who deserves it?

## PRAYER

*Father, may my desire to shine for You never transform into a desire to be the brightest one in the room. I live only to reflect Your light.*

## — 78 —

# ENJOYING THE JOURNEY

*"When you come into the land and plant any kind of tree for food, then you shall regard its fruit as forbidden. Three years it shall be forbidden to you; it must not be eaten."*

LEVITICUS 19:23 ESV

Walking by a fruit tree, you may need to watch your step. When fruit begins to appear on a tree, it soon ripens and, if not picked, falls to the ground and rots.

Even the most fruit-filled trees, however, struggle to produce fruit in their early years. During this time, it's helpful to pluck the fruit as soon as possible—not to consume it but to prepare the tree to produce large quantities of good fruit as it ages. Some experts suggest three years of this.

"Delayed gratification"—also called *waiting*—isn't a characteristic of our current culture, which wants everything fast. But as any cook will tell you, five hours spent on a home-cooked meal will produce a far greater treat than a five-minute microwave dinner.

Waiting brings the best results.

## FOR FURTHER THOUGHT

What can a Christian do to better enjoy the journey instead of impatiently awaiting the "next big thing"?

What are you being patient for? A job? A spouse? A better means of transportation? How might God be preparing you for better things through this time of waiting?

## PRAYER

*God, I know Your timing is perfect, so I'm willing to wait until my life catches up to Your plan. In the meantime, strengthen my patience.*

# — 79 —

# GOD'S *ZUGUNRUHE*

*"Even the stork in the heavens knows her times, and the turtledove, swallow, and crane keep the time of their coming, but my people know not the rules of the* Lord*."*

Jeremiah 8:7 ESV

Every autumn—in late August or early September—storks migrate south over Israel, headed from Europe to Africa. Flocks of birds such as turtledoves, swallows, and cranes follow their own interior clocks, also migrating over Israel at the same, predictable times every year. And they return every spring.

Migration instincts aren't the only things hardwired into these birds' genetic makeup—they're also keenly sensitive to the shortening of the days. In the time leading up to migration, they undergo physiological and physical changes and experience *Zugunruhe* (German for "migratory restlessness").

Jeremiah noted that while even birds took note of the changing times and returned to Israel, the Israelites often failed to acknowledge the laws of God and "refuse[d] to return" (Jeremiah 8:5 ESV). They weren't attuned to God's Word and failed to respond when He summoned them.

Let's not be like that. Let's be sensitive to God's *Zugunruhe*.

## FOR FURTHER THOUGHT

Have you ever felt God calling you to move out of your comfort zone and into an uncertain, untested future? If so, what was your response?

What would the world be like if everyone obeyed God's voice inside them as consistently as the birds obey their instincts? How can you begin building such a world today?

## PRAYER

*Heavenly Father, teach me to respond to the gentle but powerful urging that You've placed within me. May I trust Your decisions over my own opinions.*

# — 80 —

## A DRY WADI

*"But my brothers are as undependable as intermittent streams. . .that stop flowing in the dry season, and in the heat vanish from their channels."*

Job 6:15, 17 NIV

Job lived on the western edge of the Arabian Desert, where very few streams flowed all year long. Most wadis contained water during the rainy season, between autumn and spring; however, when the dry season came, the waters vanished in the summer's heat, leaving behind bone-dry channels like the dusty canals of Mars.

Job complained that his brothers and friends were as undependable as wadis. They were there for him sometimes—a modest supply of friendship and encouragement—but when he *really* needed them, in his times of deepest grief and anguish, they had nothing to offer.

It's hard to pour out to others when we feel empty

ourselves. But to take this allegory a step further, we can't just depend upon intermittent rainfall to keep water flowing in our lives. We need to be spring fed—with God as our unfailing source—so that we can always overflow onto others, even during our own dry seasons.

## FOR FURTHER THOUGHT

How do you respond to dry seasons? Does your faith continue to thrive, or do you block your last available spring and suffer in the heat?

When is the last time you offered spiritual water to someone going through a dry season? Where did *that* encouragement come from?

## PRAYER

*God, even when I feel parched and void of life, keep the stream of faith flowing. As long as You're with me, rain is always around the corner.*

# — 81 —

# TOUCH-ME-NOTS

*"The smallest family will become a thousand people,*
*and the tiniest group will become a mighty nation.*
*At the right time, I, the* Lord*, will make it happen."*
Isaiah 60:22 NLT

In the low, wet places of the woods, poison ivy abounds. Nearby, touch-me-not (or jewelweed, as it's also known) often grows. Crushed touch-me-not is a good topical first aid for poison ivy. Leave it to God to provide help just where we are likely to need it.

Touch-me-nots can actually be great fun, since their ripe pods pop at the slightest vibration. Walk through a whole patch of touch-me-nots in a boggy meadow, and something marvelous can happen: the first touch-me-nots will burst, throwing seeds farther into the patch, striking other plants. They, too, will pop at the vibration, throwing even more seeds into the meadow. Soon, seeds are flying back and forth like an uncontrolled nuclear reaction.

What a picture of God's ways! Like the tiny mustard seed that grows into a large plant, the smallest events in your life all have potential for greatness.

## FOR FURTHER THOUGHT

Can you think of a "touch-me-not"—a single, small event—that led to your salvation? What would your life be like if that event wouldn't have happened?

Have you ever considered that you might be the "touch-me-not" in someone else's life?

Knowing that all your actions—even the smaller ones—have consequences, how will this affect your behavior and your interactions with others?

## PRAYER

*God, what seems like chaos to us is a meticulously constructed plan to You. I want my words and deeds to be sparks that will light Your fire.*

## — 82 —

# EQUIPPED FOR THE TASK

*You make darkness, and it is night,*
*when all the beasts of the forest creep about.*
PSALM 104:20 ESV

Humans aren't the only ones in God's creation who work a night shift. Bobcats, mountain lions, coyotes, foxes, raccoons, and deer find it easy to prowl by the light of the moon and stars.

God made these animals' eyes with a reflective surface behind the retina, a special feature that allows them twice the use of the available light. The light stimulates the retina going in and again on being reflected out. (That internal "mirror" is why their eyes shine greenish yellow in our headlights.) In addition, these creatures' retinas give images mostly in black, white, and shades of gray—more efficient than ours in dim light.

Most of these animals don't prowl at night to avoid

humans. They're just making the best use of the abilities God has given them. Doesn't it make sense for us to use the talents and skills God has given us too?

## FOR FURTHER THOUGHT

When studying God's Word, Christians can either simply absorb the knowledge or reflect its truths in their lives for others to see. Which option are you choosing?

How does the act of reflecting God's love, compassion, and forgiveness enable us to better understand them ourselves—similar to the mirror-like retinas of those animals?

God's Spirit enables us to peer through the dark and see the shades of good and evil that lie in everything around us. How are you making use of this gift?

## PRAYER

*God, help me to be a light in this dark world, reflecting Your attributes for everyone to see—including myself. Only You can help us navigate the dark.*

## — 83 —

# THE FEEBLE FOLK

*The rock badgers are but a feeble folk,*
*yet they make their houses in the rocks.*

PROVERBS 30:26 SKJV

Rock badgers weigh six to ten pounds and, with their short ears and tails, resemble large guinea pigs. Also called hyraxes, they are found from Israel to South Africa, and as their name implies, they live in the rocks. Rock badgers' chief predators are leopards, hyenas, and especially eagles. At the slightest sign of danger, they dart into holes in the rocks—and are safe. As Psalm 104:18 (NIV) explains, "The crags are a refuge for the hyrax."

Rock badgers recognize that their enemies are stronger than they are and present a very real danger. When an eagle swoops down from the sky, rock badgers aren't so foolish as to stand their ground and prepare to fight. They recognize their limitations and seek refuge in the rocks.

We as Christians have a similar defense. The psalms state that God is our rock, our refuge, and our fortress. Like the hyrax, we are weak, but when danger is near, we can run to God, who will protect us.

## FOR FURTHER THOUGHT

How can a Christian know when to fight back against evil. . .and when to run to God for protection?

Have you ever fled when you should have fought. . .or fought when you should have fled? If so, how did that turn out? Did you learn from your mistake?

Why should Christians never seek out temptations to fight?

## PRAYER

*You've given me tools to fight evil, Lord. But sometimes, its temptations are so strong that it's best to leave it to You. Thank You for this protection.*

## — 84 —

# SURROUNDED BY SUPPORT

*Let them praise the name of the* Lord*! For he commanded and they were created. . . . Beasts and all livestock, creeping things and flying birds!*
Psalm 148:5, 10 esv

God is praised even in the behavior patterns of domestic and wild animals.

Those who deny the existence of God might say migrating geese fly in chevrons because it's easier that way. But how does every gosling figure that out on its first flight with the flock? How is it that trout, though raised on unnatural food in a hatchery, know what to eat when they're placed in a wild river?

And how do ruby-throated hummingbirds find their way across the Gulf of Mexico each fall? The males leave Texas first, then the females. Last, the young of the year set out across the five hundred miles of water. All the birds fly alone, including the young, which have never made the trip before.

Like the heavens, every part of God's creation praises Him. How? By making it obvious that God made them. We who believe God see evidence of His work at every turn.

## FOR FURTHER THOUGHT

How does knowing that God designed the internal navigation systems of a hummingbird help us understand just how much He must love us, His most prized creations?

Why do you think God created such complex natural systems when He could have just made everything simple and easy to understand?

## PRAYER

*All-knowing Lord, everywhere I look, I see complexities that could only come from You, the brilliant Creator. Thank You for assuring us of Your wisdom.*

# — 85 —

# THE GIFT OF LIFE-SAVING SLEEP

*I will both lay me down in peace and sleep,*
*for You alone,* Lord, *make me dwell in safety.*
Psalm 4:8 skjv

It turns out that animals don't just hibernate through the winter because they're lazy. Neither do they do it because everyone else is doing it or because their folks did it before them.

Scientists have discovered the blood of some creatures contains a "hibernation inducement trigger." It kicks in when daylight decreases, making the critter gather food, prepare a burrow, and go for a long snooze. If you inject HIT into other animals, they will fall asleep too.

Instincts and learned behavior are important and all, but it seems hibernating animals have been given a little extra something to see them through hard times.

God must care a lot for these creatures. He cares even more about you.

## FOR FURTHER THOUGHT

Just as He's given certain animals the tools to hibernate, God has given His children the tools to rest in Him. What are these tools?

When the urge to find solace in Your Creator kicks in, do you resist the pull or give in to it freely, enjoying the peace He provides?

## PRAYER

*Thank You, Father, for Your refreshing gift of rest. I couldn't make it through life without Your peace firmly planted in my soul.*

## — 86 —

# GOD'S LIBRARY

*And there are also many other things that Jesus did, and if each of them were written, I suppose that even the world itself could not contain the books that would be written. Amen.*

John 21:25 SKJV

Scientists have identified an estimated 2.1 million plant and animal species on our planet. That's a large number, but only a fraction of the total number of all species yet to be cataloged.

The number of stars in the Milky Way galaxy is estimated in the one hundred billion range—and that's only one of an estimated two trillion galaxies in the universe.

Earth's closest star is our own sun—a mere 93 million miles away. Its light takes about 8.3 minutes to reach the earth. The Milky Way's most distant star is approximately a million light-years away. It's hard to wrap our minds around distances like that.

The universe we inhabit is truly amazing—because our Creator God is even more so. How many books does it take to explain God and His creation? Only one—the Bible tells us everything He's deemed necessary for us to know. Someday, He'll fill in the rest of the story in person.

## FOR FURTHER THOUGHT

What questions about nature, science, or philosophy spark your curiosity? Are you looking forward to the day when God can answer all your inquiries face to face?

Why do you think God created distances so long and creatures so innumerable that it's impossible for us to traverse or count it all?

## PRAYER

*Lord, thank You for making this universe far beyond our knowledge, giving us reasons to explore Your great creation until the end of time.*

# — 87 —

# HE JUST SAID SO

*And God said, "Let the land produce living creatures according to their kinds: the livestock, the creatures that move along the ground, and the wild animals, each according to its kind." And it was so.*

Genesis 1:24 NIV

Who among us hasn't looked at the beauty and majesty of nature and wondered just *how* God did it? How did He make the mountains, the rivers, the forests? How did He set those things in motion? How does He keep them going day after day, year after year?

Without a doubt, the beginning of all things was a spectacle too awesome for our words. But the bottom line for God is that everything we enjoy in the outdoors was simply a matter of Him *speaking* it into existence.

God willingly and gladly blessed us with everything we enjoy when we spend time in the outdoors. He gave us the rivers, the mountains, the forests. . .and the time and freedom to enjoy them. How? For Him, it was just a matter of saying the word!

## FOR FURTHER THOUGHT

How does it feel knowing that the same God who spoke the universe into existence lives inside you now?

For us, creation takes a lot more than speaking. . .and a lot more resources than the nothing that God started with. Still, most of us have, in some form, the insatiable desire to create. Why?

## PRAYER

*Lord, may I never think of myself too highly. . .or too lowly. With the same voice that created the universe, You created me—and now You declare me Your child. Thank You.*

# — 88 —

# BE STILL

*"Be still, and know that I am God; I will be exalted among the nations, I will be exalted in the earth."*

PSALM 46:10 NIV

Sailing on Lake Ouachita near Hot Springs, Arkansas, is more than fun—it can be a spiritual experience.

The lake is nestled in the hills of a national forest where no homes are allowed. In autumn, the leaves of thousands of trees display a myriad of colors, revealing the handiwork of God's creative mind. It's a photographer's dream come true.

Jesus Himself—the Creator of hills and trees and lakes—appeared to enjoy the water too. He was often in a boat with His disciples, and we know of one occasion when He stilled a raging storm, making the water as calm as a fishbowl.

There's just something about water—the millions of diamond-like sparkles on its surface, the gentle slapping sound against the side of a boat, the rhythmic rise and fall of the waves. Whether we're relaxing in an inner tube on a pond or sailing at speed with a strong wind, being on the water is a peaceful, relaxing experience.

The water is a place we can still our minds and meditate on the Lord.

## FOR FURTHER THOUGHT

As seen by Jesus' calming the storm in the sea, God's power can both destroy peace and create it, depending on which side we've chosen. Which side are you on?

Sometimes, God's peace comes to us where we are—other times, God wants us to seek it, like a sailor seeking the serenity of the water. In what areas have you found God's peace?

## PRAYER

*Lord, Your power is enough to shake the earth, but it's also enough to calm my soul. Please grant me the peace I need for today.*

## — 89 —

# WISDOM FOR ALL TIMES

*As the Scriptures say, "People are like grass; their beauty is like a flower in the field. The grass withers and the flower fades. But the word of the Lord remains forever." And that word is the Good News that was preached to you.*

1 Peter 1:24–25 NLT

Watching fallen leaves swirl in the breeze of a cool, crisp autumn morning, it's difficult not to think of the cycles of life. Close on the heels of summertime's welcoming, bustling life comes a season that drives us indoors and warns of the temporary death ahead.

Our lives often mimic these seasons. The things of our lives—even life itself—sometimes feel so brief. We long to find ourselves anchored in the permanent, the eternal. And God's Word provides that place for us. Moment after moment, day after day, season after season, His Word is always there, providing an anchor for our souls.

How wonderful to know that the wisdom of the ages, given by the author of all creation, is available for those moments, days, and seasons.

## FOR FURTHER THOUGHT

Near the equator, the seasons come and go with little change. How might this resemble the soul of the Christian who stays close to God?

Have you ever gone through a life-altering, soul-crushing change? If so, how did your experience impact your journey toward where you are today?

## PRAYER

*God, in this shifting life of seasonal joys and pains, remind me of the eternality of Your promises. You are the anchor that steadies my soul.*

## — 90 —

# AN UNEXPLORED GIFT

*"But seek his kingdom, and these things will be given to you as well."*
LUKE 12:31 NIV

You might not have heard of *shinrin yoku*, but you've probably enjoyed it. The Japanese term means "wood-air bathing" and refers to the uplifting feeling you get from a walk in the woods. Studies in Japan show that trees "breathe" out compounds, half of which are as yet unidentified, that have a positive effect on our mood.

So that sense of calm well-being you get under a wooded canopy is actually a gift from the trees themselves. As well as making us feel good, it has been suggested those compounds improve health, benefiting those with diabetes and other illnesses.

We haven't really begun to explore the blessings God has infused into this world. It's conceivable that everything we could possibly need can be found in creation. So let's not spoil God's gift before we get to see how wonderful it really is!

## FOR FURTHER THOUGHT

If God placed so much beneficial material in His natural creation, how much more do You think He injected into His spiritual gift to us—the Bible?

It's been said that God has written two books: the book of nature and the book of scripture. What types of benefits can be found in both? How might some of these benefits overlap?

How are you exploring God's two books?

## PRAYER

*Thank You, God, for creating this world—and Your Word—with our needs in mind. Help me glean Your blessings out of both.*

## — 91 —

# WISE LIFE LESSONS

*He spoke about plant life, from the cedar of Lebanon to the hyssop that grows out of walls. He also spoke about animals and birds, reptiles and fish.*

1 Kings 4:33 NIV

Solomon referred to ants, bears, pigs, snakes, and dogs in the biblical books of Proverbs and Ecclesiastes. In the Song of Songs, he described several types of plants. But for the most part, his many observations have not come down to us in the Bible. So why are we told that he investigated both flora and fauna in great detail?

For one thing, as many botanists or zoologists will tell you, humans study plant and animal life simply because it's fascinating. The complexity and balance of nature convinces many of us that an intelligent designer must have been behind it.

Another reason: as Solomon repeatedly demonstrated

with his proverbs, we can draw many life lessons from plants and animals.

We may not fully understand microbiology, genetics, or other fields of science. But reflecting on creation for even a few moments leaves us in awe of God's power and wisdom.

## FOR FURTHER THOUGHT

In your opinion, what's the most fascinating object or phenomenon in nature? How does it show God's glory? What attributes of God does it reveal?

Outside of the ones mentioned in Proverbs, what life lessons can you draw from nature? What healthy attitudes and behaviors are reflected in the natural order?

## PRAYER

*Father God, You've placed lessons and inspiring truths in nature for everyone. Help me to discover and appreciate the parts of it that speak most strongly to me.*

## — 92 —

# OFF BALANCE BY DESIGN

*"I will give you rain in due season, and the land shall yield its increase, and the trees of the field shall yield their fruit."*

LEVITICUS 26:4 SKJV

God tilted the earth to give us seasons. Because the world isn't perpendicular to the sun, heat sometimes hits us straight-on and other times at an angle. Because of that tilt and the corresponding changes in the hours of daylight, nature knows there is a time to grow, a time to give fruit, a time to fall back, and a time to begin again.

Cynics might say seasons are a coincidental by-product of an "accidental" tilt. But imagine if things weren't arranged that way. The north and south would be permanently barren, and the central belt would constantly be in flower—for a while. With no chance to recuperate, how long would it take for a permanent summer to burn everything out? It just wouldn't work.

So. . .God tilted the earth to give us seasons.

## FOR FURTHER THOUGHT

Have you ever felt like your life has been tilted out of whack? Have you ever thought God might be using your skewed present to create a balanced future?

How does the story of redemption echo the theme of how God creates perfection through what most see as flaws?

## PRAYER

*Father, thank You for the seasons of the world and in my own life. Sometimes I just want stability—but You knew the seasons would cause growth.*

## — 93 —

# CHATTERBOXES

*"And when you pray, do not keep on babbling like pagans, for they think they will be heard because of their many words."*

MATTHEW 6:7 NIV

Hiking through the October woods, our boots crunch through a red-and-orange swirl of fallen leaves. Nearby, squirrels rush up tree trunks, hiding themselves on the back sides and emerging on high branches to scold us. Surrounded by the beauty of God's fall colors, these furry rodents do nothing but shoot meaningless babble our way. Their "many words" have no effect, except to prompt us to smile and chuckle.

Let's not be like squirrels. Instead of ignoring those multicolored leaves, let's praise God for them! He has splashed buckets of heavenly paint over the woods, allowing us to share in the glorious scenery.

The wise king Solomon once said, "Much dreaming

and many words are meaningless. Therefore fear God" (Ecclesiastes 5:7 NIV). Let's use our words to praise our awe-inspiring Lord.

## FOR FURTHER THOUGHT

Have you ever complained your way through a blessing? How can we as Christians make sure we never miss the good things God wants us to experience?

Are the words you speak uplifting and God-honoring, or do they tend to be mere static—distractions to be overlooked by those who seek God's beauty?

## PRAYER

*Lord, help me control my tongue. I don't want my life to become a stream of annoying background noise. May every word I speak point others to You.*

## — 94 —

# CARING FOR OUR WORLD

*And the LORD God took the man and put him into the garden of Eden to dress it and to take care of it.*

GENESIS 2:15 SKJV

Have you ever gone hiking on a new trail and arrived at an isolated Eden overlooking a breathtaking vista. . .only to find a tangle of Styrofoam lunch boxes, candy wrappers, and beverage cans strewn across the ground? A stunned question comes to mind: "If people love this beautiful spot enough to come here, why do they trash it?"

The answer is that they really don't care. True, they're moved by the view of wild beauty, but their worldview is so self-centered that once they've enjoyed something, they don't care how they leave it. They don't have the *big picture.*

As Christians, God expects more of us.

The first commandment God gave to mankind—even

before "Be fruitful and multiply"—was to care for the earth. God didn't placed Adam in the paradise of Eden just to enjoy the garden's awesome beauty. Adam was also to "tend and keep it," preserving and nurturing its beauty for future generations. Let's do the same.

## FOR FURTHER THOUGHT

How do many Christians treat God's gift of salvation like those careless hikers treated the beautiful landscape?

How can we make sure that our appreciation of God's beauty doesn't devolve into selfish exploitation and hoarding?

## PRAYER

*Lord, give me a heart that craves the act of sharing good things with others. I never want Your outpouring of blessings to stop with me.*

# — 95 —

# CLOSE TO LIFE

*And He said to me, "It is done. I am Alpha and Omega, the beginning and the end. To him who is thirsty I will freely give of the fountain of the water of life."*

REVELATION 21:6 SKJV

The highest waterfall in the world is one of creation's most astonishing sights. Venezuela's Angel Falls drops 3,212 feet in total, the water generally turning to mist long before it reaches the base. It's not easy or cheap to see this amazing site, though. Hardy adventurers must fly by plane, travel by car, then hike for an hour to view the beautiful wonder.

Many people go to great lengths to enjoy this unusual waterfall. But the greatest wonder of all is ours for the taking—God's water of life. He *wants* us to experience it, and He doesn't require a long, costly trip to obtain it. The distance between our knees and the ground is all we need to cover to drink the water of life.

## FOR FURTHER THOUGHT

How often do you "travel" to God's throne to receive His forgiveness?

Are you as eager to seek God's will as those travelers are to see Angel Falls? Why?

## PRAYER

*Lord, I'm amazed by how easily Your water of life is obtained. Help me to never take this life-changing gift for granted.*

## — 96 —

# THE CUTE ALLIGATOR

*Do not be deceived: God cannot be mocked.*
*A man reaps what he sows.*
GALATIANS 6:7 NIV

Zoos often stage informative programs for children, allowing the kids to get to see exotic animals up close. Sometimes, they even get to touch or hold the creatures.

In one zoo, the keeper produced a baby alligator from a case. "Cool!" came the cry from the boys in the audience. Meanwhile, the girls called it "cute." Everyone got a chance to touch the gator as the handler held it, keeping both the kids and the animal safe. During his talk, the zookeeper informed the kids that this "cute" baby gator would someday be a ferocious fourteen-footer.

Sin's a lot like that. What begins as a small, seemingly "safe" indulgence soon mushrooms into an unstoppable threat. We may think we have things under control, but before long, our sin is too big to handle. Often, by the time we realize the danger, it's too late.

The next time temptation comes calling, think of the baby alligator.

## FOR FURTHER THOUGHT

Have you ever engaged in a "harmless" pastime that soon turned out to be anything but? If so, what lessons did that experience teach you?

Why do you think some people choose to adopt "baby alligators," even when they know what they'll become?

How can a Christian spot a potential temptation? What do the danger signs for various sins look like?

## PRAYER

*Father, help me flee sin, even when it's a baby and its teeth look like they couldn't hurt anyone. Sin is sin, and it will always be deadly.*

## — 97 —

# PRAYER OF A SHRIVELED LEAF

*And we all fade as a leaf, and our iniquities, like the wind, have taken us away. And there is no one who calls on Your name.*

Isaiah 64:6–7 skjv

Fall, with its swirling colors and chill air, can be a beautiful and invigorating season. Still, there's something melancholy about a faded leaf scuttling down a dark street, driven by a biting wind.

If we are the leaves, God is the tree. Sin not only severs our connection to the life of God, it rips us loose and drives us away down empty streets. Sadly, when we reach such a state, we're usually no longer even praying for help.

Yet even in such a desperate condition, we *can* cry out to God. In the very next verses, Isaiah prays for mercy: "Yet you, Lord, are our Father. . .do not remember our sins forever. Oh, look upon us, we pray" (Isaiah 64:8–9 NIV).

Are you in that state? Or are you still attached to the tree but about to drift away? Do you need God's presence renewed in your life? Pray. . .*now*.

## FOR FURTHER THOUGHT

It takes a strong gale to snap a healthy leaf from a tree. What are some winds in your life that threaten to cut you off from God? How can you remain attached to Him?

When is the last time you prayed? How healthy is your attachment to your life-giving God?

## PRAYER

*Father, may I recognize when my connection with You is growing weak. I never want to drift away on the winds of fear and sin.*

# — 98 —

# DEEP BLUE SEA

*There is the sea, vast and spacious,*
*teeming with creatures beyond number—*
*living things both large and small.*
PSALM 104:25 NIV

Only within the last few years have scientists been able to capture a live giant squid on camera. Occasionally, creatures thought to be long extinct are found living and thriving in the oceans. It's been suggested that there are more unknown, never-before-seen creatures living in the ocean than there are creatures we've identified. In many ways, it seems we know more about the surface of the moon than we do the ocean floor.

God has given us a wonderful world to explore, and as we learn more about this planet and everything in it, we can't help but marvel. Will we ever reach full understanding of every creature God has created? That's unlikely. His creation is far beyond our full knowledge.

That's the kind of God we serve—deeper than the oceans, more varied than the life they contain. And yet He knows each one of us intimately!

## FOR FURTHER THOUGHT

Science has been described as the act of "thinking God's thoughts after Him." Given that God's thoughts are infinite, how long would it take us to discover it all?

The scientific method is built on not knowing—ignorance breeds curiosity, which breeds discovery. How might the same be true for our spiritual life?

## PRAYER

*Almighty God, I know I'll never catch up to Your genius. Thank You for permitting Your creations to uncover tiny pieces of Your ultimate plan.*

## — 99 —

# HE SPEAKS TO US EVERYWHERE

*Bless the* Lord*, O my soul! O* Lord *my God, you are very great! You are clothed with splendor and majesty, covering yourself with light as with a garment, stretching out the heavens like a tent.*

Psalm 104:1–2 esv

North of the forty-fifth parallel, you'll sometimes see the night sky come alive with flashes and streaks of color cutting across the inky, star-speckled blackness. These "northern lights" are technically known as the aurora borealis.

In North America, the most common colors are greens and blues. Sometimes, we get only a brief glimpse. Other times, they hang motionless for a few minutes then collapse or seem to slide away.

Auroras hold our attention as would a great waterfall—

which they occasionally resemble. They can appear as curtains on a stage, waving slightly as if in a light breeze.

Scientifically, we understand how particles in the solar wind interact with Earth's atmosphere and magnetic field to produce these shifting lights. But it's a privilege to watch God stretch out those "tent curtains" for our enjoyment.

## FOR FURTHER THOUGHT

The ancients looked into the sky in awe over these mysterious wonders; now, we know exactly what causes them. How does that make them even more amazing?

What other, less dramatic "light shows" does God put on throughout nature? How often do you take the time to enjoy them?

## PRAYER

*Lord, beauty is everywhere—from the tundra in the north to the tropics in the south, and everywhere in between. Thank You for Your glorious, inescapable presence.*

## — 100 —

# IT'S ALL FOR YOU!

*Come and see what God has done,*
*his awesome deeds for mankind!*
Psalm 66:5 niv

Many people—Christian or not—can believe that God created the natural world they see around them. But what some, even followers of Christ, don't understand is that creation itself is an expression of God's love for humankind.

A well-known Christian leader who happens to be an avid bass fisherman once marveled, "It's amazing to me that God loved me so much that he made these slimy little creatures. . .just so I and my friends could enjoy them!"

The diversity we see in creation—the differences in the world's lands and waters, as well as the variations God placed in the animals, birds, and fish—is a testament to the Lord's creativity. But it's also a testament to the lengths God is willing to go just to demonstrate His love for each of us.

Next time you're enjoying the outdoors, don't forget to personalize your gratitude for what God has created. . .just for you!

## FOR FURTHER THOUGHT

God planned everything for your eyes to see. How does knowing this impact your attitude toward life's small blessings?

How can we look for personalized beauty in God's creation without lapsing into self-centeredness? How can we share the wonders of nature with others as well?

## PRAYER

*Father, only You could design unique blessings for everyone on earth each day. Open my eyes to the wonders You've prepared for me.*

# MORE GREAT DEVOTIONS FOR MEN

Charles Spurgeon, "the prince of preachers," is well remembered and remarkably readable some 130 years after his death. Now, this devotional for men has been compiled from his decades of weekly sermons. You'll find deep yet accessible teaching on biblical manhood, as Spurgeon distills godly principles for men of all ages.

Hardback / ISBN 978-1-63609-719-0